CATALINA IN THE MOVIES

BY LEE ROSENTHAL

WINDGATE PRESS : SAUSALITO, CALIFORNIA

Movie set at the Isthmus, Catalina Island, c.1935

ISBN 0-915269-24-4

WINDGATE PRESS
P.O. Box 1715, Sausalito, CA 94966

FIRST PRINTING
Printed in Korea by Sung In Printing America, Inc.

SAILING along Catalina's coastline, one easily can dream of faraway places. Even the names suggest wondrous lands; Little Gibralter, China Point, Italian Gardens, Cabrillo Harbor, and, of course Avalon, the mythical island valley of King Arthur's time described in Tennyson's *Idylls of the King*. Inland, the place names take on an old southwest flavor; Rancho Escondito, Cactus Peak, Black Jack Mountain, and Silver Canyon. It's easy to see Catalina Island in many guises, as a stand-in for other places. Movie location scouts saw that straight away. Between 1915 and 1935, the golden age of Catalina movie-making, part or all of over 150 Hollywood movies were filmed on Catalina. The movies ranged from short slapstick comedies to major studio productions like *Mutiny on the Bounty*. In recent decades Catalina has been the locale for countless videos, television shows, commercials, and background for scenes for major studio productions such as Roman Polanski's *Rosemary's Baby* and *Chinatown*.

FOR Hollywood's budding movie industry around 1915, Santa Catalina Island, a mere twenty-odd miles distant from the mainland, was a godsend. Film making was breaking out of studio confines as audiences demanded more variety, more outdoor adventure and scenery. The melodramas and two-reel comedies cranked out weekly by the studios were getting stale. Movies needed scenes shot "on location" to provide a fresh look. Westerns could be shot in the still unpopulated hills immediately behind Hollywood. And the streets of Los Angeles provided outdoor settings for car chases and urban outdoor scenes.

But exotic ports of call were another matter. If a movie company needed Hong Kong, or the South Seas, or the Riviera, location shooting presented a major problem. Profitable as they might be, movie companies could scarcely afford to pack up a crew and send it half way around the world, even if they could corral a group of actors and production people long enough for the trip. Aside from cost, production schedules wouldn't allow for the travel time. Studios had to complete a film in days and weeks, not months. Shooting in remote or distant locations was impractical.

The solution, to put it bluntly, was fakery. Or, as Hollywood would spin it, "creating magic." Convenient nearby locations, dressed with appropriate props, became foreign lands. The studio "backlot" was born. The "lot" was just that, empty real estate usually next to the production facilities, fenced in for security. Within the bounds of the back lots, sets could be built to represent almost anywhere, with varying degrees of success. But elaborate sets needed for the illusion of grand scale could run up costs too. And low-budget sets usually looked low budget.

By 1918, Los Angeles and vicinity had become populated enough to create visual hindrances for movie makers who broke out of the back lots. At the beaches, crowds quickly gathered around the cameras. Telephone wires in the background popped up among the swaying *papier mâché* palm trees. Streetcars, motor cars, and other visual distractions rattled into the scene when least expected.

Above left, Little Harbor on Catalina's windward coast resembles Greek islands in the Aegean Sea. Below left, Greek ruins built above Isthmus Cove on Catalina for MGM production *I Live My Life*, 1930, starring Joan Crawford and Brian Aherne.

Catalina Island provided an exception. The island, then as now, was sparsely populated, with most of its fifty-four mile coastline unmarked by the trappings of civilization. No overhead wires, few roads and no automobile traffic. Much of the island, clothed in sagebrush, cactus, and chaparral, appeared generic enough to resemble many places, with a little work, almost any place. And Catalina, only an hour or two by boat from San Pedro was isolated enough so that cast and crew, once on the island, could be kept together.

Everyone making movies in Hollywood in the 1920s and 1930s spent some time at Catalina. And it's a good bet that more than a few scenes were shot on Catalina just to provide an excuse to be there.

Apart from movie making, the island was well known to movie people. In the days before air travel became commonplace, sunny Catalina was an ideal respite from the hectic pace of Hollywood. Southern California possessed many charming hideaways where the stars could slip away unnoticed. Catalina was one of them and its appeal proved irresistible. The calm easygoing tempo of Avalon and the natural beauty of the island made a day or two away from the studio seem like a two week holiday. Secluded beaches and coves along Catalina's coastline provided convenient anchorages for those interested in things other than fishing. The fishing, of course, was unsurpassed, and hunting still was permitted in the Catalina hills. The locals took movie star sightings in stride and, for the most part, respected their desire for privacy.

Top right, director Cecil B. DeMille assisting Wanda Hawley, in costume, for scene in *Male and Female*, starring Gloria Swanson, Catalina, 1919. Below, DeMille's set at the Isthmus, Catalina Harbor side, representing Jacob's Well in biblical Syria for *The Ten Commandments*, 1923.

Film crews and actors working on the island often returned to play. Some became habitues, their names, faces, sailboats and yachts familiar to residents. These included Charlie Chaplin, Paulette Goddard, Clark Gable, Errol Flynn, Humphrey Bogart and Lauren Bacall, and John Wayne. Everyone making movies in Hollywood during the 1920s and 1930s spent some time at Catalina. And it's a good bet that more than a few scenes were shot on Catalina just to provide an excuse to be on the island.

Catalina proved ideal for underwater photography, her clear waters revealed spectacular flora and fauna. And the Isthmus became known in the industry as an ideal "South Sea Island" location. In the 1950s and 1960s, television competed with the movies for an audience. Catalina again rose to the occasion, providing television camera crews with highly photogenic backdrops for commercials, serials and made-for-TV movies.

Today, with advanced film making technologies such as computer animation, demand for background shots on Catalina is diminished. Few American-made movies are shot entirely on location. Most are a combination of studio sets, background location shots, and skillful editing. Cameras can and do go anywhere, making the whole world a movie location. Still, Catalina Island appears regularly in the movies and on television, perhaps not in a starring role, but as part of the supporting cast or even as an uncredited extra. Part 3 of this book is devoted to "The List," a compilation from several sources of the major movies made, at least in part, on Catalina Island. With over two hundred and fifty movies from 1910 to the present, the list is a work in progress, unlikely ever to be encyclopedic. Many early movies have been lost or exist as fragments. Many other movies contain brief unidentified shots of Catalina that only the sharpest eye could detect. After all, part of Catalina's charm lies in her easy and convincing transformation on film.

Right, United Artists' stars and moguls who helped shape movies in the 1920s and 1930s were familiar faces on Catalina. In this 1930 photograph are, left to right, Al Jolson, Mary Pickford, Ronald Coleman, Gloria Swanson, Douglas Fairbanks, Joseph Schenck, Charlie Chaplin, Samuel Goldwyn, and Eddie Cantor. Backdrop, the Catalina Island Country Club golf course.

MOVIE MAKERS GUIDE TO CATALINA

1. William Wrigley, Jr. residence, Mt Ada
2. Catalina Country Club
3. Hotel St. Catherine
4. Hamilton Cove
5. Middle Ranch Junction
6. Gallagher Beach
7. Long Point
8. Italian Gardens
9. Black Jack Mountain
10. Middle Ranch Dam
11. Eagle's Nest
12. Mt. Banning
13. Mt. Orizaba
14. Airport In The Sky
15. Cabrillo Harbor
16. Empire Landing
17. Ben Weston Beach
18. Lobster Bay
19. Mt. Torquemada
20. Wells Beach
21. Fourth of July Cove
22. Cherry Cove
23. Bird Rock
24. Ship Rock
25. Howland's Landing
26. Whale Rock
27. Silver Peak
28. Emerald Bay
29. West Point
30. Eagle Rock

Catalína in the Movíes

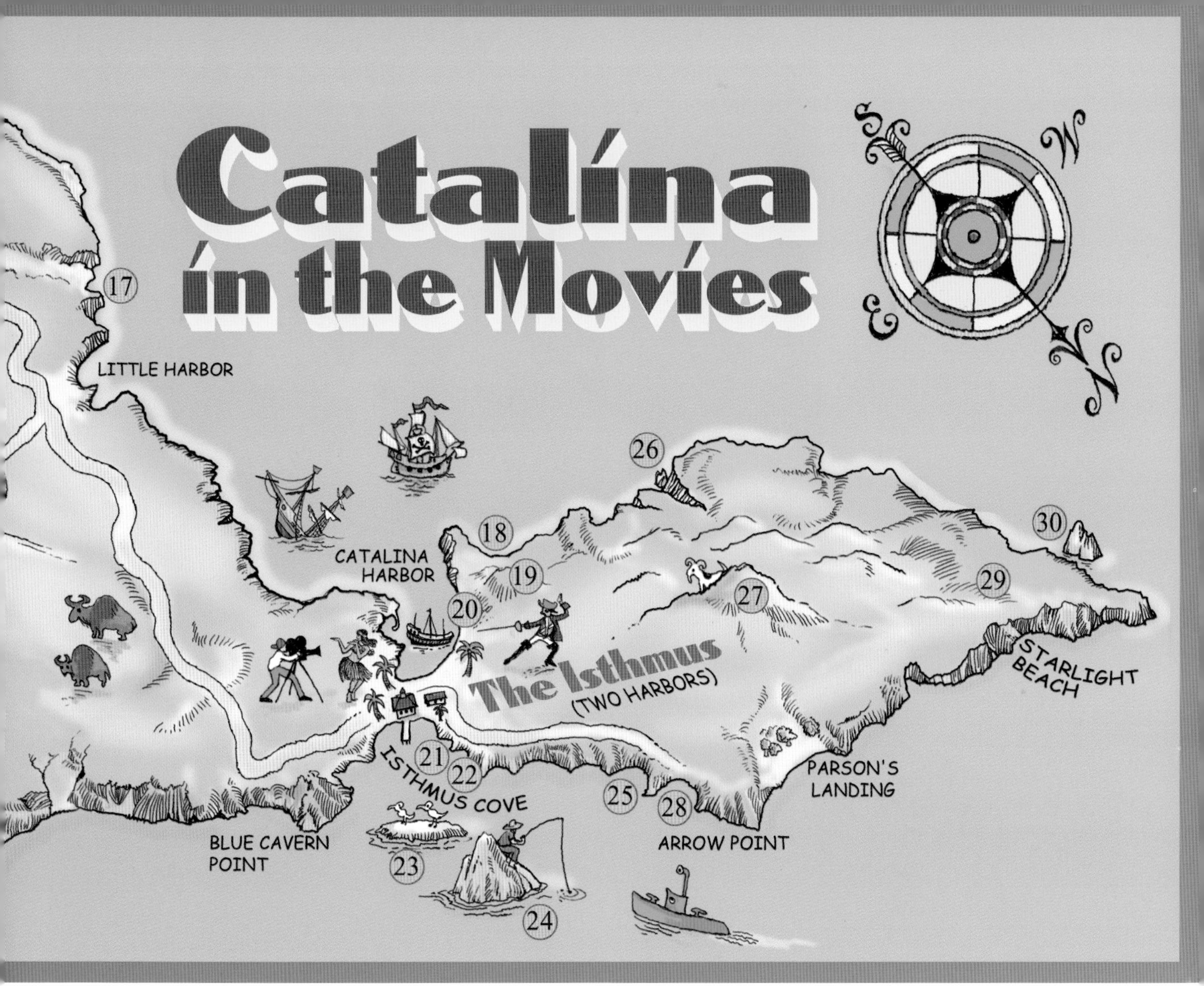

CATALINA MOVIE TIME LINE

1896

In Chicago, Thomas Edison first projects moving pictures on a screen. Seen as a novelty.

1898

Tuna Club founded on Catalina, first sport fishing club in America popularizes big game fishing with rod and reel.

1900

Nickelodeons open in storefronts across America. Catalina's Isthmus becomes popular with boaters, fishermen and divers.

1902

First commercial wireless station established in Avalon connects island communications to the mainland.

1908

Writer and actor David W. Griffith directs his first movie, innovates and expands the new medium.

1910

First motion picture shot on Catalina Island: *Feeding Seals at Catalina Isle.* Length is less than ten minutes.

(*Continued on Page 98*)

Mack Sennett bathing beauties pose on a Catalina beach, 1915. These and other similar photos sold by mail order helped promote his movie series called *Mack Sennett's Comedies*. They promoted Catalina Island too.

"Old Ben" Catalina's First Film Star

Sometimes known as Big Ben, he stood out among Catalina's sea lion colony in the late nineteenth century. Larger than most, the grizzled bull elbowed, or flippered, to the front of the pack each day as fish scraps were fed to the seals. He was bold, friendly, and ate more than most. He willingly posed for photographs and established himself as a Catalina regular by 1900. Swimmers often recalled Old Ben swimming alongside them and performing for the beach crowds, begging handouts, shuffling along Crescent Avenue. A veteran of countless snapshot sessions, Old Ben broke into the movies when Mack Sennett and his comedy troupe came to Catalina in 1915 to film *The Sea Nymphs* with Fatty Arbuckle and Mabel Normand, The 1915 postcard, above left, showing Old Ben with five-year-old Bernice Cameron was seen by millions worldwide. In time, Old Ben's visits became less frequent. His last verified sighting was in 1921, although unsubstantiated sightings continued for some time. A statue of Old Ben was dedicated in Avalon in 1975.

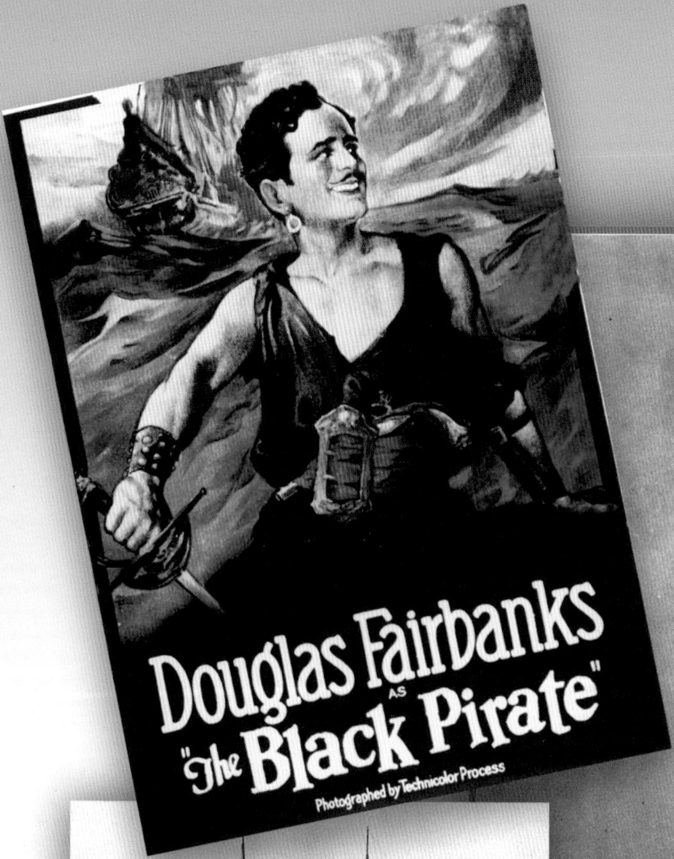
Douglas Fairbanks
AS
"The Black Pirate"
Photographed by Technicolor Process

Pirates of the Magic Isle

CATALINA made an ideal "pirate island." Over a dozen pirate and sea adventures were filmed at Catalina from 1916 through the 1930s, including two versions each of *The Sea Hawk* and *Treasure Island*. The rogues above and Douglas Fairbanks at left are from *The Black Pirate*, 1926, the first Technicolor movie shot on Catalina. Far left, old sailing vessel *Santa Clara* converted to "pirate" ship for the 1924 silent movie *The Sea Hawk*. Movie studios drew from classic tales by Robert Louis Stevenson, Rafael Sabatini and others, and modeled their pirate costumes on the illustrations of Howard Pyle, example at right.

Catalina as the Wild West

COWBOY movies on Catalina Island? Surprising as it sounds to some, the island's mountainous interior lends itself well to scenes of the Old West. The absence of roads and overhead power lines creates an unchanging rugged vista. The color photo below shows an area today near Blackjack Mountain, little different from the same neighborhood in 1898, top, opposite page. Prior to 1918, when the Banning family owned Catalina Island, stage coaches regularly made the trip from Avalon to the Isthmus. In the 1920s, the old coach and stage road appeared in westerns filmed on location on Catalina.

Catalina's famous bison that roam freely on Catalina descend from twenty-four animals brought to the island for the 1925 western movie *The Vanishing American*, with Richard Dix.

Hollywood's Playground

Hollywood came to Catalina to work, liked what it found, and stayed to play. Like most others, movie stars enjoyed sailing, fishing, swimming, and basking in the sunshine. Some came for seclusion offered by Catalina's hideaway coves and beaches, others for the carefree activity of Avalon. In the 1930s, stars glittered in the new Casino ballroom, danced to music of the big bands, and partied on private yachts moored in Avalon Bay.

THE Catalina Island Yacht Club, below, opened in 1927, became a home away from home for visiting yachtsmen. Actor Lee Tracy, right, at the helm of his sailboat in the late 1930s. Below right, United Artists' Joseph Schenck, in yachting cap, welcomes guests aboard his yacht *Invader* at Avalon; actor Ben Lyon, Norma Shearer and, with hands in pockets, her husband Irving Thalberg, production chief of MGM,

Hotel

ST. CATHERINE

E. H. BERNEGGER, MANAGER

DINNER

BAKED CHEESE CANAPE

CHILLED CELERY RIPE OLIVES SPICED BEETS

SOUP

PUREE LEGUMES CONSOMME ALPHABET

FRENCH BREAD GRAHAM BREAD HOT ROLLS

FISH

BAKED CATALINA BARRACUDA, ANCHOVY SAUCE

POTATOES BRABANT

ENTREES

CURRY OF PACIFIC COAST SHRIMP WITH RICE

BROILED DEVONSHIRE LAMB CHOPS WITH BACON

COMPOTE OF CALIFORNIA PEACHES WITH PISTACHIO

ROAST

PRIME RIBS OF NATIVE BEEF AU JUS

CATALINA ISLAND DUCKLING, APPLE SAUCE

Built in 1918, the Hotel St. Catherine set a high standard of elegance for Catalina and became first choice of most visiting Hollywood celebrities. Some, however, found more privacy by slipping quietly into the Atwater or the Glenmore Hotel in Avalon. The private pier at the St. Catherine in Descanso Cove allowed famous guests to come and go by boat without facing the Avalon summer crowds. Below left, Edna May Oliver and director Lloyd Corrigan in the St. Catherine dining room during filming of RKO's *Murder on a Honeymoon*, 1935.

The Hotel St. Catherine served as backdrop for the 1924 Cecil B. DeMille production, *Feet of Clay.* Right, stars Vera Reynolds and Ricardo Cortez. Below, a crowd scene from *Feet of Clay*, Miss Reynolds, lower right, and the hotel in full splendor. Far right, the promenade from the Hotel St. Catherine led to the Casino and to Avalon around the point. Insets: Top, Bonita Granville and Jackie Cooper on the hotel dock, c.1947. Bottom, Orson Wells and Dolores Del Rio load up for a yacht party. She starred in the 1932 David O. Selznick production, *Bird Of Paradise*, with scenes shot on Catalina.

EARLY western star Tom Mix, an avid fishermen and yachtsman, lived in Avalon in the 1920s. His house today still bears his brand. Above, Mix's yacht *Miss Mixit*, Avalon Bay, and at left, he poses with daughter aboard her namesake boat, *Thomasina*. Tom Mix filmed several short western adventure films on Catalina's interior hills.

Right, entertainer Al Jolson, who in 1927 starred in the first "talking" movie, *The Jazz Singer*, casts his line at Avalon. His hit recording of "Avalon," written in 1920 boosted the island's popularity.

OPERATIC EDITION
AVALON
Song
Lyric & Music by
Al Jolson &
Vincent Rose
Jerome H. Remick & Co.
NEW YORK
DETROIT

Leo "Duke" Fishman, legendary Avalon life guard, movie stunt man and actor from the 1930s to the 1970s, chummed with Hollywood folks: top left, Fishman with Mickey Rooney, top right, John Wayne, bottom left, Henry Fonda and Ward Bond, bottom right, Tony Curtis and Marilyn Monroe during filming of *Some Like It Hot*.

Stars at play in the 1930s. Clockwise from above, Jimmy Durante, Paulette Goddard and husband Charlie Chaplin, Lupe Velez at the Isthmus, and James Cagney.

Some celebrities were avid fishermen, some just liked to pose with big fish. Right, Bing Crosby and his marlin, 1934. Crosby was on Catalina for *We're Not Dressing*, a Paramount musical with George Burns, Gracie Allen and Ethyl Merman. Below left, visiting Winston Churchill and his catch in 1929. Below right, actor Warner Baxter and his nineteen-pound bluefin tuna.

Top, "Our Gang" and their catch at Avalon, 1925, while filming one of their comedies for Hal Roach. Below, Victor McLaglen and his barracuda haul on Avalon's pleasure pier.

While movie stars often came to Catalina aboard their private yachts, they also traveled to and from the island aboard the famous steamers *Catalina* and *Avalon*, and to the Isthmus from Avalon aboard the *Cabrillo*, left, and *Blanche W.*, center left. The *Catalina*, below, is escorted into Avalon Bay by the *Miss Catalina* speedboats. Impatient stars and studio executives flew to and from Catalina in the 1930s on the seaplanes from the Catalina Airport at Hamilton Cove.

Below, William Wrigley, Jr. and Charlie Chaplin aboard the SS *Catalina*, c.1928.

Left, Sid Chaplin, Charlie's brother, and the first air service to Catalina, 1919.

Catalina Airport at Hamilton Cove, 1930s.
SS *Avalon*, below.

THE Isthmus, above, site of most movie-making activity on Catalina Island. Isthmus Cove, near side, and Catalina Harbor across the narrow land bridge, around 1940. Below, Isthmus Cove today. Opposite top, a movie "jungle" set at Isthmus Cove in the 1930s sharing space with supply tents and recreation facilities. Below right, the Cove from the pier around 1938. Main building at the left in the photo is Christian's Hut, legendary movie-star hangout left over from Clark Gable's quarters when MGM filmed scenes here in 1935 for the movie *Mutiny on the Bounty*.

Catalina--
the Isle of Romance

And adventure, too, in the eyes of movie makers. In the 1930s America's past as a seafaring nation still resonated with movie audiences. Hollywood drew on history as well as fiction, recreating accurate vessels, costumes and sets. Sea adventures, tales of heroism and tragedy, lent themselves well to Catalina's medley of pristine waters, rugged cliffs, and sun-washed beaches, unchanged since the days of Juan Cabrillo and the Spanish *conquistadores*.

AMONG the most popular adventure movies filmed on Catalina was the 1926 silent film *Old Ironsides*. It features a sensational sea battle off "Tripoli," below, between the USS *Constitution* and the Barbary Coast raider *Algiers*. The scene, filmed at Catalina's Isthmus, used full-sized retired sailing vessels rebuilt as early nineteenth-century warships. The *Algiers* also played the captured American frigate *Philadelphia* in the same movie and was burned in Catalina Harbor for a climatic scene. *Old Ironsides*, first "big budget" movie shot at the Isthmus, received glowing reviews and played to full houses. The hospitality and cooperation shown Famous Players-Lasky by the Santa Catalina Island Company while filming *Old Ironsides* established Catalina as a first-rate movie-making venue.

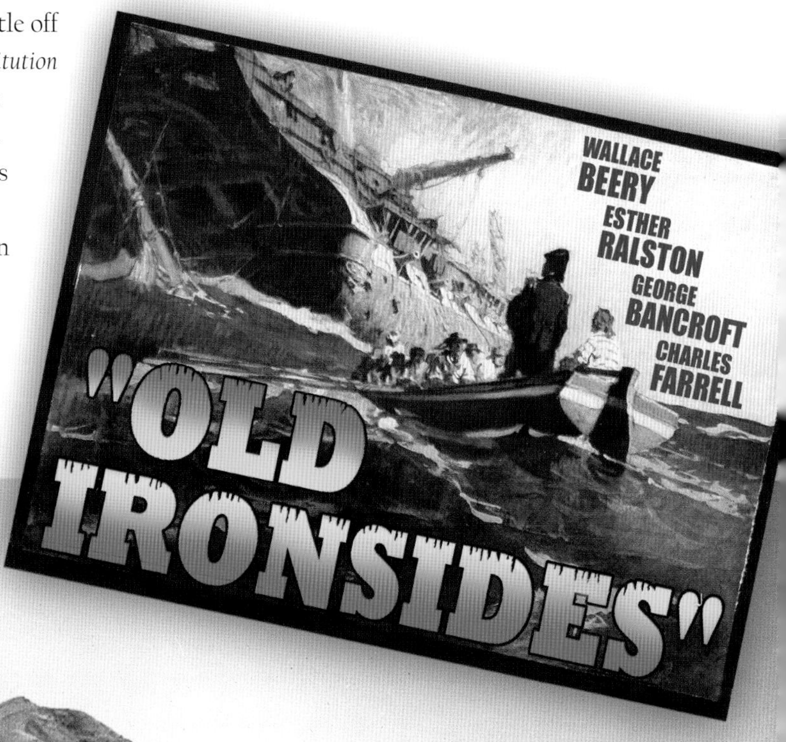

Above, Catalina Harbor today, Ballast Point in the foreground, reveals no trace of the movie sets of the 1920s and 1930s. Geographically, however, little has changed. Below, the same area in 1926 with actors costumed for *Old Ironsides*. Barges like the one in foreground were loaded with equipment and supplies on the mainland and towed to Catalina by Wilmington Transportation Company tow boats.

Below, a prop man rests a stack of *papier mâché* canon balls on his lap at the Tripolitan fort, seen at bottom, far right, near Ballast Point.

Above, actors in costume at Catalina Harbor. The turbaned man facing left is Boris Karloff before his rise to fame as Dr. Frankenstein's monster. Below, inset, director James Cruze instructs crews of his fleet by radio, the first use of radio communication in movie production.

Set of Jean Lafitte's pirate stronghold for the 1938 movie *The Buccaneer*, White's Landing, Catalina.

THE ultimate pirate story, Robert Louis Stevenson's *Treasure Island*, appeals to film makers as well as audiences of all ages. The 1934 version, filmed at Catalina Harbor and Emerald Bay with Jackie Cooper as young Jack Hawkins and Wallace Beery as the villainous Long John Silver, has become a classic. Metro-Goldwyn-Mayer wanted to film in Hawaii but director Victor Fleming became entranced with Catalina and persuaded the studio to film on the island. The close proximity of Catalina to Hollywood paid off when Wallace Beery's wife became ill during the filming and Beery, an accomplished pilot, could fly home each night to be with her.

TREASURE ISLAND

Above right, Jackie Cooper, between takes. Below, pirate Richard Powell spins a tale for cast and children of cast members, left to right, Jackie Cooper, Johnnie Dinsmore, Madeline Powell, Richard Powell, and Ottilie Kruger. Exotic birds from the Catalina Bird Park were enlisted as movie extras to add authenticity.

ONE of the most ambitious movie projects ever involving Catalina took place in the summer of 1935. *Mutiny on the Bounty*, made by MGM, starring Clark Gable, Charles Laughton and Franchot Tone, was based on Charles Nordhoff and James Hall's famous novel of the same name. The film was to be shot entirely on location in Tahiti, but things didn't work out that way. MGM sent an expeditionary crew to Tahiti and background shots were filmed. The film company in Tahiti built full-scale 18th century villages and employed 2,500 native South Sea natives as extras for the movie. When the crew returned to Hollywood, they found 50,000 feet of film underexposed and unusable. A second crew was dispatched to Tahiti to reshoot most scenes, while Catalina filled in for others.

Right, Catalina residents, among many used as extras in *Mutiny on the Bounty*. Below, blocking out a scene at Catalina Harbor aboard the replica ship *Bounty*.

More than 600 cast and crew came to Catalina for additional filming. Six native villages were built at various coves around the island as well as a reconstruction of England's Portsmouth Harbor for the movie's opening scenes. Footage was shot on San Miguel Island, miles north of Catalina, as well as at the real Pitcairn's Island in the South Pacific. Near San Miguel Island in heavy seas, a camera barge capsized, killing an assistant cameraman and injuring several other crewmen. Additionally, over $500,00 worth of camera equipment went to the bottom.

The movie cost nearly $2,000,000, an enormous amount for 1935. After all the production trials and tribulations, *Mutiny on the Bounty* opened to acclaim and won an Academy Award for best picture of 1935.

Below, director Frank Lloyd, left, gets a smile from Movita as Franchot Tone and Clark Gable look on.

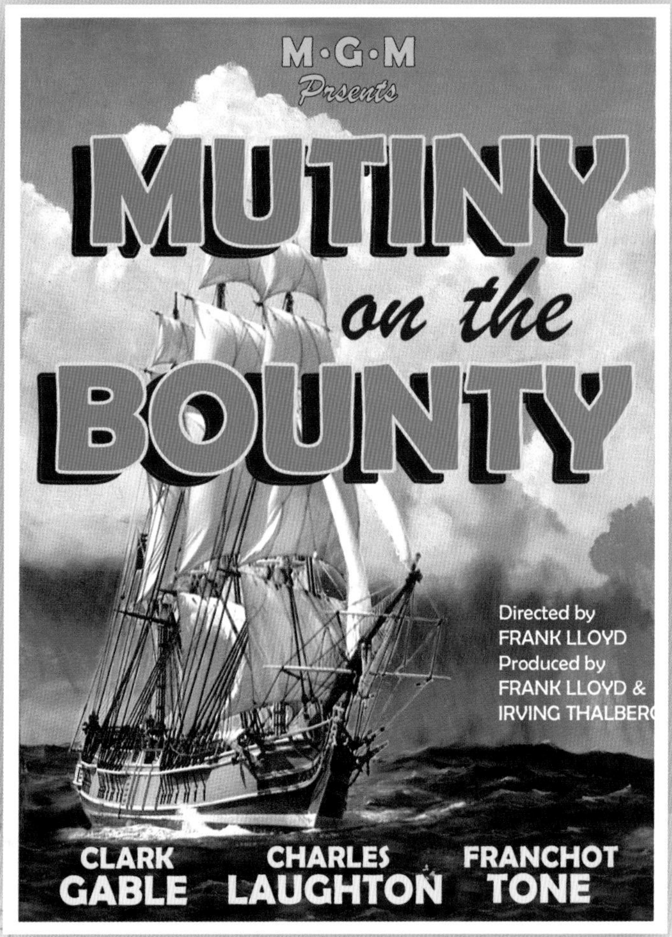

Three replicas of the original *Bounty* were constructed. A full-size version was sailed to Tahiti and the second, built on the stern of an old schooner, was used for interior shots and closeups. A third scale model of the *Bounty*, eighteen feet long, was towed to Catalina to be wrecked and burned for the movie. Under tow to the island in heavy seas, the scale model broke free of the tow line with two men aboard. The Coast Guard rescued the men and boat two days later. Reportedly, producer Irving Thalberg, hoping the MGM crew could find the missing men, delayed notifying the Coast Guard because he didn't want negative press for the upcoming movie.

Below, movie ships at Catalina Harbor for *Mutiny on the Bounty*. One vessel, the old schooner *Samar*, has only a reconstructed stern, used for exterior close ups. The full-scale *Bounty* is at right foreground. Other vessels represent the British fleet at Portsmouth Harbor. The multi-striped three-masted ship is the *Balclutha*, restored today as part of the San Francisco Maritime National Historical Park.

Above, legendary "Christian's Hut" in the late 1930s. This Isthmus landmark began as Clark Gable's sleeping quarters, upstairs, and saloon downstairs, during the filming of *Mutiny on the Bounty*. Named for Fletcher Christian, Gable's character in the movie, the building later was used by other movie people and boaters and as a movie set. The Hut burned in 1940 along with the Isthmus dining hall. See pages 27 and 33.

The 1962 MGM remake of *Mutiny on the Bounty*, with Marlon Brando in role of Fletcher Christian, was not filmed on Catalina. Brando, however, was on Catalina in 1965 for *Morituri*. He stayed in an apartment in Avalon while co-star Yul Brynner helicoptered home to Los Angeles every day after filming.

Right Eighteen-foot-long model of the *Bounty* "wrecked" on the rocks for the 1935 movie.

AMONG the old sailing vessels reconstructed as movie ships in the 1920s and 1930s, the old schooner *Lily* became the *Bounty*, the *Llewellyn J. Morse* became *Old Ironsides*. Some movie ships had multiple roles. The sailing ship *Metha Nelson*, for example, was used in *The Sea Wolf*, 1930, *Seas Beneath*, 1931, *The Painted Woman*, 1932, and finally, the old workhorse in 1939 became the *Falcon* for *Rulers of the Sea*, with Douglas Fairbanks, Jr. More than a few movie ships were burned or blown up for special effects, often off Catalina Island. At right, the *Falcon* lies at San Pedro with a miniature version of the vessel alongside to starboard to be used for certain scenes. Below, Gary Cooper and George Raft get fencing instructions aboard the *Kaiulani* disguised as a slave ship for *Souls at Sea*, 1937. After World War II the old ships were gone and movie studios had to build ships from scratch, one reason why fewer seafaring movies were made after the 1950s.

FALCON
GREENOCK

Catalina's ever-popular glass-bottom boats have appeared in movies and served as camera platforms for underwater photgraphy. Below, publicity shot for MGM's *The Glass Bottom Boat*, 1966, starring Doris Day and Rod Taylor.

Glass bottom boat *Princess* in the 1950s

Left, one of ten Adventure Tours "shore-boats" in Avalon Bay, with the Catalina Yacht Club in background. These work-horse boats taxi visitors to and from their vessels, and are used by movie companies for hauling crews, lights, and camera equipment. One boat, for example, was used for the movie *Jaws* to drag the giant shark fin through the water.

Below, submersible used in filming TV commercial, c. 1960.

Below, Catalina Adventure Tours yellow semi-submersible, *Nautilus*, introduced in 1999, had a small part in one of the first "Fear Factor" TV episodes, shot in Avalon in 2001. The company has provided various services for the movie industry for feature films such as *Jaws, The Last Voyage of the Valhalla, MacArthur, The Parent Trap,* and *Grey Lady Down.*

William Wrigley, Jr.,left, with David M. Renton, c.1928.

CATALINA IN THE MOVIES

Part 2: How William Wrigley, Jr. and David Renton Brought Hollywood to Catalina

"There is no reason why the Isthmus cannot be made a real place for the movies."

—*David M. Renton, 1929*

AMONG the first motion pictures produced by Thomas Edison, inventor of the movie projector, was *Feeding the Doves*, a fifty-foot long "one-reeler." The Edison Manufacturing Company described it as "a farm scene, showing a young girl and her baby sister throwing crumbs and grain to the doves and chickens." Hardly Academy Award material, but this was 1896, and movies were in their infancy. Early cinematographers pointed their cameras toward anything that moved. After all, these were movies, and paying customers wanted to see things move.

Apparently, *Feeding the Doves* proved a money maker and a new movie genre was born. Edison produced a sequel in 1901, called *Feeding the Pigeons*, and followed the next year with *Feeding the Bear at the Menagerie*. Other studios joined the band wagon with a succession of one reelers such as *Feeding the Dogs*, *Feeding the Elephants*, and *Feeding the Pigs* (filmed on location in Ireland in 1898). Ducks, otters, llamas and even a hippopotamus soon starred in their own "feeding" films.

A decade later, the genre still could draw an audience. In 1910, Essanay Film Manufacturing Company produced a little ten-minute epic called *Feeding Seals at Catalina Isle*. This marked the beginning of Catalina's career in the movies. The following year, film maker Hobart Bosworth produced a film about whaling with scenes shot at Catalina. Perhaps other films around this same time included Catalina scenes but, if so, their history as well as their footage is lost to us.

Pioneer director David Wark Griffith was the first to take advantage of Catalina's geography rather than its wildlife. In 1912, he directed for Biograph *Man's Genesis*, with scenes shot on the island. Director and actor Hobart Bosworth returned to Catalina in 1913, where he shot key scenes for *The Sea Wolf*, the first authorized film rendition of Jack London's classic work. Jack London himself appeared at his desk in the opening shot. The following year Bosworth filmed the second in his series based on Jack London's popular novels. This time, for *The Valley of the Moon*, Catalina was a location as well as San Francisco, Carmel, and Jack London's ranch in Glen Ellen, north of San Francisco.

By this time other studios knew about Catalina's diverse and versatile terrain and seascape. Vitagraph shot scenes for *Captain Alvarez* on the island, a movie supposedly set in Argentina. Producer Mack Sennett, famous for his "Keystone Cops" comedy two-reelers, came to Catalina in 1914 with Roscoe "Fatty" Arbuckle to film *The Sea Nymphs*. Sennett came back the next year with Sidney Chaplin, brother of Charlie Chaplin, to make *A Submarine Pirate*. The actual submarine, borrowed from the Navy, was filmed in San Diego. Sid Chaplin supervised elaborate underwater scenes shot off Catalina.

Another submarine picture, *Civilization*, shot in 1915 and released the following year, contains unique Catalina footage. Produced by Thomas Ince, a Hollywood pioneer who developed the early western movie format, *Civilization* involved a fantasy kingdom, a doomsday submarine, and an anti-war theme. In November, 1915, fire swept through Avalon, destroying about half of the town including the Hotel Metropole. The movie company filming *Civilization* nearby quickly moved their camera to Avalon and shot the burned city. The scenes of devastation were incorporated into their movie.

Before and after the fire, Avalon appeared as the backdrop for dozens of two-reel comedies besides those of Mack Sennett's Keystone Mutual Company. And why not? Avalon, blessed with a glittering harbor and picturesque hillsides bathed in delightful sunshine, projected a playful spirit. The island of romance. Avalon made an ideal setting for boating, yacht parties and beach romps. Avalon could take on a dramatic face too, as in *When A Man Sees Red*. In 1917 Fox made this violent tale of shipwreck, revenge and murder, with scenes of Avalon representing a South Seas port.

The World Film Company in 1916 decided to make a "South Sea Islands" picture. Director Harry Pollard, in search of a suitable location, visited Catalina and scouted the coastline. This is probably the first instance where Catalina served as a South Seas island, an often repeated role in the following two decades. The movie's working title, *A Pearl of Paradise*, was changed, and the final title is not recorded.

While Catalina's many rock-bound coves and hidden small beaches make good sites for seafaring adventures, nothing on the island can match the Isthmus for South Sea atmosphere—with the help of a few well-placed fake palm trees. The Isthmus, that narrow strip of land near the west end pinched between two picture perfect harbors, possessed many desirable features for film making. The dramatic joining of land and sea is both sublime and spectacular, with steep cliffs climbing from jagged rocks on one hand, and flat beaches gently rising to graceful low hills on the other. In the harbors photogenic rocks jut from clear blue-green waters. Because the two harbors face opposite directions, varied natural lighting conditions exist. Vegetation on the surrounding hills is sparse, so that almost any terrain from desert to forest can be simulated. The general absence of roads and other man made "improvements" on the hills kept them pristine for the camera's all-seeing eye. And, perhaps most important of all, the Isthmus was relatively isolated. Not only did this keep crowds of onlookers from interfering with filming, it kept the film crews from running off to various diversions.

By 1919 the South Sea Island shipwreck/castaway device was becoming *cliché* in film melodramas, yet it was a money maker for the studios. Famous Players-Lasky, for example, brought a crew of two hundred to Banning Beach in 1919 to produce a South Seas picture called *Terror Island*. The Isthmus had become so popular with movie companies that remnants of movie sets and assorted pieces of abandoned props and equipment cluttered the area. Several deliberately wrecked and burned vessels dotted the coastline of Catalina, primarily at Two Harbors. Along with the historic Banning House and the Civil War barracks, ramshackle buildings and tents, a small hotel, restaurant and bowling alley catered to the yachting and fishing crowd.

The Santa Catalina Island Company controlled commercial activity on the island and apparently granted permission to movie studios to use the island with little supervision. But that was about to change. The Banning family, owners of Catalina Island, had fallen on financial hard times. The Company never fully recovered from the big Avalon fire of 1915, and, by 1919, the island was for sale. The real estate firm of Blankenhorn and Hunter formed a group of investors and purchased Catalina from the Bannings. The major shareholder was William Wrigley, Jr., legendary businessman and entrepreneur, best known for Wrigley's Chewing Gum. After visiting Catalina for the first time shortly after the purchase, Wrigley was so charmed by the island, he bought out Blankenhorn and Hunter to become sole owner.

William Wrigley, Jr., no idle dreamer, said, "While my motive in purchasing the island is largely a romantic one, I am going to leave no stone unturned to make it a refuge from worry and work for the rich and poor." He envisioned Catalina as a vacation paradise and, to that end, eagerly welcomed visitors and made improvements catering to their needs. William Wrigley, Jr. also wanted returns on his investments. Setting in motion a construction and development program for Catalina, he wanted simultaneously to generate revenue and preserve the island's natural setting. Wrigley recruited David M. Renton, a well-known Pasadena builder, to be general manager of the Santa Catalina Island Company. A new era for Catalina in the movies had begun.

As much as William Wrigley, Jr. might have wanted it, he did not live full time on Catalina. He built a summer home above Avalon, but his business interests kept him mainly in Chicago. With David Renton in charge of myriad projects for Wrigley, a regular weekly correspondence began between the two men. It continued for the next twelve years until William Wrigley, Jr.'s death in January, 1932. Renton then corresponded with Wrigley's son and heir Philip K. Wrigley. The correspondence between David Renton and William Wrigley, Jr., and later Philip Wrigley, documents the island's development history between 1919 and 1934. While the movie business occupied only a part of their correspondence, it demonstrates the trusting and productive relationship between William Wrigley, Jr. and David Renton. Wrigley visited Catalina when time permitted. Renton worked from Avalon. The motion picture business was unknown territory for them but they sensed the opportunity that the movies might be good for Catalina. And, both men being imaginative and creative, they no doubt found it fascinating.

In the early 1920s they began to promote Catalina Island as a filming venue for major movie studios. Filming benefitted the Company in three ways. It generated publicity for the island; the movies sets and the filming became a unique tourist attraction; and the expenditures by the movie companies while filming generated revenue for the Company. The first reference to the Hollywood studios in their correspondence occurs in May 1924, when the Famous Players-Lasky Moving Picture Company came to Avalon to film *Feet of Clay*, a Cecil B. DeMille production. Renton wrote, "This is going to give

us a tremendous amount of publicity. [It] will feature the Hotel St. Catherine and the beach considerably. The name 'Catalina' as I understand it will enter into the story and be mentioned frequently in the sub-titles." He also noted the other aspect of catering to the movie people. "We made a flat rate of $6.50 per day for all the stars at the Hotel St. Catherine. The Atwater made them a rate of $2.00 apiece, per room, which is responsible for our big increase in revenue."

An additional dimension to filming at Catalina involves David Renton's sons, Malcolm and Arthur Renton, ages sixteen and twelve respectively in 1924. Between 1920 and 1924, at least two dozen movies were shot on Catalina, including pirate epics, undersea adventures, dramas and slapstick comedies. Film crews and movie stars, common sights in and around Avalon, also worked near Middle Ranch and the Isthmus. Tom Mix, the biggest cowboy star of the day, maintained a home in Avalon and frequently made short films on the island. Not surprising then, that the young Renton boys would have developed a keen interest in movie making. They asked their father for a motion picture camera, and got it, in the spring of 1924. The camera, a used 35 millimeter Pathé model, was suitable for professional work.

David Renton mentioned the camera to Wrigley. "Saturday afternoon we went up the road and shot some scenes of the dam and of the water coming over the summit into the canyon. As soon as I get the films developed I will send them back to you so that Phil [Philip K. Wrigley, William Wrigley, Jr.'s son] can put them on the screen."

Wrigley wrote back, "I am very much enthused over the motion picture camera that you have bought for Malcolm and Arthur. A moving picture history of the doings and goings-on at Catalina Island will be a mighty interesting thing to have and it can be added to each year. I don't know why I overlooked this fact myself. The boys will have a lot of fun and do a good work at the same time."

One of the first documentary assignments the boys gave themselves was filming the launch at Wilmington, May 3, 1924, of the SS *Catalina*, the Company's new steamer destined for service between Avalon and the mainland. Within the next few days they sent the film to William Wrigley, Jr. Wrigley wrote to Renton, "The SS *Catalina* films arrived and I have seen them run twice in my office on a daylight screen. I want to congratulate Malcolm on his success. We had another showing of the Renton Brothers' *Catalina* films last night at Phil's house. It gave us all quite a 'kick.' It is remarkable that Malcolm should make such a good start with his first use of the camera. I like to look at these pictures and at the same time they make me homesick. There is more fun in Catalina Island in one day than there is here in a month."

Renton shipped off another film by Malcolm showing the maiden voyage of the *Catalina* and the Forth of July crowds and events at Avalon. Delighted, Wrigley wrote, "The only fault we have with the film is that it was just one-tenth as long as we wished it was." Over the next several years as Hollywood companies filmed on Catalina, the "Renton Brothers" filmed island activities for William Wrigley, Jr.

The most popular "location" with Hollywood movie companies on Catalina continued to be the Isthmus. Not surprising since, in the 1920s, South Sea Island and pirate adventure pictures remained in fashion. Only a handful of people lived full time at the Isthmus. Among them were the Greigs, William and Frances, who managed the concessions there catering mainly to fishing and boating activities. Wrigley made the Isthmus a regular stop for the steamer *Cabrillo* on her daily voyages to and from Catalina. Visitors could go ashore, sample Mrs. Greig's home-cooked meals and return to Avalon either by steamer or motor stage.

Renton saw possibilities that would make the Isthmus even more favored with the movie crews without disrupting other visitors. The few permanent buildings, such as the old Civil War barracks and historic Banning House, could serve as accommodations for the crews. He made other improvements, a dining hall and kitchen, staffed by Santa Catalina Island Company employees. Other amenities included bathrooms with showers, storage sheds, better tents, and a larger dock for barges from the mainland loaded with equipment.

Since the film companies wanted to shoot in good weather, a regular film-making season was established, from spring through fall. During the season, film crews from various studios would reserve the Isthmus facilities, the dining hall, cabins and dormitories, tents and supply buildings. They would arrive, sometimes by the hundreds, set up shop, build sets and props, block out scenes, and begin filming. Each company might stay on location for a few days to several weeks. When one company completed shooting and departed, another followed close behind and the process would repeat. Sometimes work by two companies overlapped.

After operations ceased in the fall, buildings and equipment were repaired and made ready for the next season. Movie props and sets left behind were stored for future use. Frequently new buildings were added during shut down, and infrastructure such as water, sewer and electricity service improved. A skeleton crew manned the Isthmus through the winter until spring, when the staff again expanded to meet the needs of incoming film crews.

Use of the Isthmus as a location was free. The Santa Catalina Island Company made money by providing at reasonable cost, room and board, special catering, transportation and other services. Other opportunities emerged. As a master builder and owner of a lumberyard in Pasadena prior to moving to Catalina, David Renton knew the value of lumber. The movie studios frequently found it more effective to leave on the island materials used in filming, including vast quantities of lumber, rather than ship them back to the mainland. Renton capitalized on the lumber trade, buying from one movie company and selling to another. And he accumulated used props and sets left behind and leased them to subsequent film crews.

Catalina's famous buffalo herd originated from this practice. In December, 1924, Tom White, representing the Famous Players-Lasky Film Company, brought fourteen buffalo for use the following spring in filming *The Vanishing American*, a Zane Grey western epic. Whether or not the buffalo were ever filmed for this or any other movie remains a mystery–they are not mentioned in the script and do not appear in the finished movie. Perhaps the movie should have been called *The Vanishing Buffalo*. When the movie company finished their project, the buffalo were left behind, set free to roam the hills. Renton and Wrigley saw the small herd as a movie asset and, over the years let the herd increase, even acquiring more animals. Today, descendants of these buffalo find little movie work but enjoy Catalina's grassy hillsides.

Demands on Renton's time grew as movie making activity on Catalina Island increased. As vice president and general manager of the Santa Catalina Island Company, David Renton already had his hands full. His charge from William Wrigley was to make Avalon into a first class seaside resort. Among other things, he supervised transportation on the island and the Wilmington Transportation Company, which operated the tugs, barges, and cross-channel steamers. Renton had already built the Atwater Hotel, the Sugar Loaf Casino, a new wing for the Hotel St. Catherine, and upgraded the water and sewer systems and the power plant. In addition, he was about to embark on mining operations, a brick and tile factory, the Bird Park, and the new Casino. In their letters, Renton and Wrigley referred to the people involved in the motion picture business as "movies." And dealing with the "movies" presented a challenge. They were demanding and apt to be temperamental. Certain directors and actors required "special handling." Because the studios employed many people at great expense working long hours, they required and expected efficiency. They were prepared to pay a premium for often super human efforts required by the Company to meet their needs. One of the Company's needs, Wrigley and Renton determined, was a person who could deal with the "movies" on a regular basis and speak their language.

In 1926, the movie-making concession at the Isthmus was turned over to Tom White, a dynamic movie producer and entrepreneur from Los Angeles (who had brought the buffalo to Catalina). White had close contact with the Hollywood studios and industry personalities. A charismatic hard worker, he had creative ideas and unique foresight. White would manage the operation and receive a percentage of the proceeds, thus freeing David Renton to concentrate on other island business. A big part of White's job, of course, was to boost Catalina as a location to the major Hollywood studios. One of his first accomplishments and a major coup was persuading Paramount/Lasky Film Corporation to film the "big budget" silent movie *Old Ironsides* at Catalina.

Wrigley was pleased. Over the years, he spent a good deal of his personal fortune making improvements on Catalina Island, often with little or no financial return. Whenever an activity showed promise of paying its own way, he welcomed it.

As filming for *Old Ironsides* got under way, David Renton checked in at the Isthmus from time to time. He wrote to Wrigley in April, 1926. "The 'movies' are still at the Isthmus. On account of heavy fogs they are spending considerable money. Believe they are using from 400 to 500 [crew and extras]. We expect to derive considerable revenue from this picture and we will be well repaid for the little damage they do."

The following month he wrote, "I was down to the Isthmus last week and made arrangement with Tom White to the effect that we would wreck all of the Paramount/Lasky sets and temporary buildings and place the grounds in good shape when they conclude their picture. In return, we will receive the large amount of good lumber at no additional cost. This is a good piece of business for us when one considers that our tugs, barges, derricks, and everything connected with the [Wilmington] Transportation

Company is deriving considerable revenue there from. Tom White's concession will also be greatly benefitted, and the publicity the Island will receive is not to be ignored."

William Wrigley liked what he heard. Enthusiastic about the new venture with Tom White, he responded to Renton," It would be a fine idea if the Lasky people could make a large picture an annual event, provided they did all the work on Catalina Island."

Old Ironsides with its spectacular sea battles off Catalina, opened to big audiences and good reviews. Renton proudly wrote to Wrigley," "I am enclosing the film pictorial section of the *Los Angeles Times* for your perusal. This, as you will note, covers the filming of *Old Ironsides* at our Isthmus. Without a doubt, Catalina Island will derive a tremendous amount of valuable publicity from this super-film."

Tom White took David Renton to see *Old Ironsides* in Hollywood during Renton's visit to the mainland to buy lumber at San Pedro. "It certainly is a wonderful picture," Renton wrote, "although I am not an expert judge along those lines. One thing I noticed is that they had a capacity house. It seemed very odd to see Ship Rock and Bird Rock looming up in the picture."

Encouraged by his own success, Tom white proposed even bolder plans to Wrigley and Renton. He wanted to film various locations on the island to show prospective movie studio "clients" as an inducement. And he proposed producing movies himself on Catalina for general release and distribution. His new venture would be called Catalina Sea Pictures Corporation. Wrigley and Renton gave careful consideration to his plans.

Wrigley wrote to Renton, "What you say about Tom White's enterprises rather enthuses me. If we can arrange it so that he can make some money out of the proposition and we will get additional business, I am strong for it."

Renton wrote, "White now has his permit for selling stock. He is very much pleased with his prospects. They are going to put on real western movies and cut out the 'flapper' style of picture which doesn't amount to a whoop and is cluttering the market. In this connection he has lined up two big companies, Universal and Metro-Goldwyn. That should create considerable work for our tugs. Understand in that respect that tug charges per day for movie work has gone up to $300.

"The Lasky people have a big farm [on the mainland] where they have all types of sets which a great many companies use. They, of course, probably make more pictures than any other one company on the west coast. White's proposition will probably be along the same lines. White's company [will] impress upon the various movie companies that they can make just as good pictures on Catalina as anyone else and just as cheaply.

"White knows this game from bottom to top; knows all of the stars and producers and distributors and furnishes many of the principals for the important prologues in and around Los Angeles, that he would be well adapted to handle this situation successfully and in the manner we wish." The "prologues" produced by White were live vaudeville opening acts that, in the 1920s, preceded feature silent movies in larger movie theaters.

"He is a real live wire," Renton continued, "a regular 'showman' and he seems to sense what the public wishes and will pay for. Naturally, like all the 'movies,' he is a trifle temperamental but he is a quick thinker and very capable. If you see fit, I will take up the proposition with him and see what we can work out. I believe it would help out our Isthmus and Avalon sections at the same time."

About this time in 1927, Wrigley acquired the Riviera Theater in Avalon. White proposed improvements. His new company would bear the cost in exchange for a year's lease. Wrigley wrote to Renton, "It's a strange thing we never thought of Tom White in connection with our movie theater. I think it will be a fine idea if you can make a deal with him. If Tom White is interested in it we will have a real first class place. It certainly was run down towards the end of my visit and that theater really represents us. The whole outfit looked cheap and was cheap. One of these days we will make Tom White Vice President in charge of the Movie Industry. Do you know how Tom is making out in getting money enough to start his own picture factory?"

Renton replied, "Have been watching Tom White's place on the mainland and everything seems to operate with plenty of 'pep.' He is acquainted with and controls a great many of the vaudeville stars and I do not think he is going to worry very much about another theater coming in here. White has already ordered a new organ that will give the people some real music instead of the second hand affair they now have. I am confident we are doing the right thing in giving White this chance. He is entitled to a year's lease at least since he intends to put considerable money into the affair. With the various prologues that White intends to stage, it will provide variety, put us on the map and insure success." Wrigley to Renton: "I have every confidence in Tom White. Please give him a year's lease."

By May, 1927, the renovated Riviera Theater in Avalon was ready. Renton informed

Wrigley. "White's theater will probably be opened up this coming week. Tom has a big feature picture lined up, probably *What Price Glory*. The decorations are very fine, along Spanish lines. Fine draperies in the panels on the walls. Everything is decorated in wonderful shapes and colors. The organ will be installed complete and ready for the opening night. Music is a big factor in [a theater's] success. White has changed the seating capacity to 630, which adds about forty more seats. He also plans to run a comic picture show in the summer, when the crowd is here between 11:00 and 12:00 at night."

A week later, the big opening of the Riviera Theater took place. Renton wrote, "Very sorry that Mrs. Wrigley and you were not present for the opening. Buying a pipe organ, installing it and having it running in six days, redecorating the whole theater—which makes it second in beauty only to Grauman's in Los Angeles—dying the old carpets and installing machines, changing all the seats, all in about two weeks is quite a job. I had to bear the [financial] brunt of a good portion of the whole proposition. In fact, the last piece of work was put up two minutes before 7:00 PM. Had a full house and a wonderful show. Our Gang Comedy and *The Fire Brigade* were shown. Everybody seemed to be elated at the new theater's appearance and also with the show."

Meanwhile, movie production at the Isthmus and around Avalon continued. In the fall of 1927, White suggested some costly improvements to the Isthmus. Until then, electric power needed by the movie companies had been provided by portable generators. Renton to Wrigley: "Tom White has been inquiring about a real power line to the Isthmus. Had our man survey same and make up an estimate. Of course, if Tom ever blew up we could have it on our hands for our own use entirely, but believe no doubt in the future it will prove an advancement and asset anyway."

Wrigley wrote back, "If the power line could be run to the Isthmus it looks to me like it might be a good investment. Tom might blow up but the Isthmus will always be a good place for movies."

Renton reported, hinting that the new power line might even extend the movie-making season. "The Fox Film Company came in today with a barge load of equipment; furniture, generators, and about everything necessary to make films. The generators are sent over to leave at Sugar Loaf for an emergency. In the event they don't have sunshine, they will use them for a substitute. However, we have had a wonderful week of sunshine here—beautiful October weather."

Two weeks later, Fox completed their project. Renton wrote, "Another company came in yesterday with a barge-load of equipment to film some sort of Egyptian picture at Sugar Loaf. They have tents and old wagons, bears and donkey, and everything that might enter in a picture of this type. [This could be a scene from C. B. DeMille's *The King of Kings*] I imagine they should be here for a week or more. Certainly glad to be able to get such companies as they leave nice revenue in our hotels—it keeps our employees busy and helps the town all around."

The following spring saw the "movies" back again for a film at Avalon. They built sets along the beach near the Tuna Club. Renton wrote, "We have a bunch of Fox Company movie folks taking films along our board walk. [Probably for *Seventh Heaven.*] They have a great many hot dog stands erected along the walk and many people were enquiring as to whether we had gone into that business too."

Plans at this time were underway to replace the Sugar Loaf Casino, the ballroom that Wrigley had built in 1920, with a new larger and much more grand structure. The new Casino would house a circular ballroom for up to 6,000 dancers above a 1,184 seat movie palace, the Avalon Theatre. Tom White felt strongly that the new movie theater within the Casino should accommodate sound films, which in 1928 seemed to be the wave of the future. He urged Renton and Wrigley to install a sound system and mentioned Vitaphone, proprietary sound system of Warner Brothers. Renton apparently had misgivings but Wrigley flat out opposed the idea.

He wrote to Renton, "In reference to Tom White's suggestion that we put the Vitaphone sound system in the new theater, I would not do this under any circumstance. The Vitaphone is used in several theaters in Chicago but they are the cheaper class and mostly controlled by Warner Brothers. I visited one of the theaters twice and as far as I am concerned, the Vitaphone spoiled the rest of the entertainment.

Undeterred, White found another sound system. He persuaded Renton that the Kellogg sound system he had in mind for the new Casino was superior to Vitaphone. Over the next year as the Casino was being built, White continued to push for sound equipment. Renton wrote to Wrigley, "Note what you said about the 'talkie' moving pictures. I have seen but two or three and didn't think much of them. White claims, however, that next year there will be no production of silent pictures. In fact, the Fox Company [already] is not making any more of that type."

Wrigley reluctantly yielded and allowed the installation of a sound projection system. Still, he didn't like the new medium. In 1929 Wrigley said, "I have only heard one 'squawky' and that was in New York at one of the largest theaters. I stood it for twenty minutes and then went out and walked in the rain for amusement."

Renton set up a compromise for the new Casino. "The 'talkie' equipment Tom White intends to have operating on the opening night may be all right and may be all wrong. I told him it would be a good plan to have a silent picture available as well as the 'talkie' in the event anything went wrong."

Renton kept Wrigley up to date on the progress. "We are putting the [Casino] Theatre in fine shape, and are ready to turn it over to White. With his new Kellogg system he is putting in for the 'talkies,' if it works out, he will probably be a very rich man as White has a big interest in it with Kellogg's son. This system is the simplest one on the market. The synchronizing of film and voice is the clearest of any I have heard."

In his enthusiasm, White apparently persuaded Wrigley to install a film processing lab in the Casino so that movie film shot on Catalina could be developed and viewed by producers and directors without returning to the mainland. Although built, the facility was never used as intended. Renton kept a close eye on White's expenses and hinted to Wrigley that all may not be well with White's other enterprises. "He is certainly running very close to the line on cash. We will put in a special auditing system and demand a special bank account from him for our share of the receipts."

Renton and White invited William and Cecil B. DeMille to Catalina to get a preview of the Casino theater and its sound system. Renton fired off the DeMille's reactions to Wrigley, certain it would ease Wrigley's apprehension.

"Mr. William DeMille stated 'it is amazing that Mr. William Wrigley, Jr., who is not a theatrical man, should be the first man to have built *THE* theater we have been praying for. The credit for this achievement alone will be worth all the effort and great expense. Mr .Wrigley has done what every producer of sound pictures has been hoping could be done. The Catalina Casino is the first theater auditorium that has been built for sound pictures and in my tests I have found it to be absolutely perfect in its acoustics.'

"Mr. Cecil DeMille is most enthusiastic over the illumination and color effects in the theater. The projection room and its facilities for previews most especially appeal to him. Both DeMilles state there is not another theater in the world that approaches it."

The Casino grand opening took place on May 29, 1929. [*The Iron Mask*, Douglas Fairbanks, was shown in the theater.] Renton described the event to Wrigley. "White has worked very hard during the past month in an endeavor to get the 'talkie' affair working satisfactorily. We did all the work; furnished all the equipment, and installed it. At the last moment he was under such tension that I detailed a man to just stick with him all through the performance to calm him down a little. It pleased me very much to see everything go along as nicely as it did. It was a perfect opening I think."

Apparently, White insisted on showing only "talkies" at the new Casino, and the sound system caused problems as Wrigley had predicted. Renton wrote to Wrigley, "White has more ideas than any other man I have ever seen. Some of them are very good and some of them are ridiculous. He likes to do a little experimental work with other people's money. From now on I am going to show him how to run this place. If he had taken your advice and mine about running the silent pictures until such time as they had perfected the 'talkies' so that they are synchronized instead of the voice running ahead of the pictures, or the pictures running ahead of the voice, it would have been better for everyone concerned."

Wrigley responded. "Tom has spent all the money he ever made on his big ideas and quite a good deal of the money I've loaned him. Personally, I like him and it's fine to have a man with ideas, but when the man has the ideas and we have the money, we have to stop, look and listen."

Despite their concerns, Wrigley and Renton stuck by Tom White a while longer, although clearly his star was in descent. White's movie production company, Catalina Sea Pictures Corporation was in financial trouble. His leases on the Isthmus facilities expired in 1928 and were not renewed by Renton and Wrigley. As Renton said of him, "He has lots of ambition, but does not use good judgement at times." In August, 1929, Renton wrote to Wrigley, "Tom White had another bad check come thorough the bank which they would not honor."

He pointed out to Wrigley that perhaps, given White's financial troubles with his movie enterprises, it was time to strike out in a new direction. Referring to the theater and Isthmus movie concessions, he said "We can take over ourselves. We have enough movie companies at the Isthmus to cover expenses and no doubt make a little profit."

Within two weeks, Renton wrote to Wrigley, "Fired Whittle [Tom White's part-

ner] at the Isthmus. He is absolutely no good. If satisfactory to you, we can operate the Isthmus ourselves. We know many movie outfits. Without a question, we will have to install talking pictures in the Theater. Talking pictures are in their infancy, however, the public seems to want and demand talking pictures and attends them strongly."

Wrigley turned the Isthmus over to Renton, saying, "When a movie company wants to come over they can hunt up [our] movie people to give them permission, and said people will be you." Tom White was out of the picture.

Renton energetically took up the flagging enterprise at the Isthmus. Within days he was able to report to Wrigley, "I'm having a movie company come over today to stop at the Hotel St. Catherine. There are forty-three in the party, good business just when we want it. They will stay four or five days. Also had a call from another movie outfit [Famous Players-Lasky] that has been over here before and liked our treatment of them. The manager is coming over tomorrow to line up a possible location at the Isthmus or thereabouts for a picture. We will get them alright, they know we are running it now."

Renton assured Wrigley that the Isthmus operation was in good hands. In late 1929, Paramount Famous Players-Lasky came to Catalina to film *Dangerous Paradise*, based on Joseph Conrad's *Victory*. When the Lasky movie company was due to arrive, Renton wrote, "We're going to give these fellows something good to eat this time and see if we can throw off the curse of past dealings at the Isthmus. Whittle served them ant paste instead of syrup, which made the 'movies' a little sick. Fortunately, nobody died.

"There is no reason why this Isthmus cannot be made a real place for the 'movies' and do some good business, and next year we can advertise the use of the Banning Cottage which will house twenty-five persons. We can buy and book better pictures than Tom White. While I think Tom is honest, his gears are out of mesh."

Within a week, in late September, Renton could report, "The Banning Cottage is furnished and in very good shape. I am having the old dance hall fixed up so the 'movies' will have space for entertainment; playing cards, or whatever they wish. It might be a good plan for us to turn the old [Civil War] barracks into dormitories. We would be better equipped to take care of sleeping accommodations for the lesser help, rather than putting them up in tents full of holes, which have about served their time.

"I found out there are very few 'movies' who would come to the Isthmus anymore if White was connected with it. I had no idea that so many were sore at him.

"After the Lasky outfit is all through with the sets, we will secure the lumber back which we sold them, and then sell it two or three times more to other movie outfits and still have it when they are through!

"We have the MGM troupe over here at present filming a sea picture [*The Single Standard*, Greta Garbo]. They seem to be very well pleased. After endeavoring to take pictures up and down the coast [near] Santa Rosa Island, they find their cost is less here and they can work less hours—better weather—and keep their players together easier.

"Also there are a great number of fake South Sea Island palm trees at the Isthmus. They are really worth nothing, but are thirty feet long, so rather than ship them away, we are going to rent them to the 'movies' at $5.00 per day."

Renton then suggested another way to generate some revenue from the Isthmus movie operation. "While we must spend a little money in painting and placing the whole affair in shape, I do not see why we cannot, in addition to handling the 'movies,' have visitors going on the Isthmus trip too. We can also rent the Banning House and other spots to visitors who like quietness and this beautiful county at the end of the island. There are a number of sets at the Isthmus which we are leaving intact as they are very interesting to many visitors from the East. Also, we have the carpenter shop of Jesus Christ used in filming *The King of Kings*. It doesn't look great but it is an attraction."

Wrigley was satisfied with Renton's new management at the Isthmus. He wrote, "I feel very sure that when the 'movies' find out that you are running the Isthmus, and the Santa Catalina Island Company is back of everything we may do, we will have much more business than we have had lately. You are absolutely right in fixing up the place to make it look like the rest of our property. I like your idea of making a dormitory. The best lumber business in the world is down at the Isthmus. It is the only place I know where we sell lumber six or seven times and still have it."

Renton kept Wrigley up to date on the routine goings-on at the Isthmus. In early October, 1929, just before the stock market crash, Renton wrote, "We have 140 'movies' up there including quite a number of stars. One of them, who gets paid $25,000, held up the whole cast last week by complaining about a little sore throat. [This was either Samuel Goldwyn's *Condemned*, starring Ronald Colman, or first National's *The Isle of Lost Ships*, starring Jason Robards.] Have rented three trucks and three touring cars to them, and a good number of old palm trees. We have twenty 'movies' in the Banning House

at $8.00 per day and lodging about 130 of them at $5.50 per day in the barracks. We secured $5,000 from the other company which just finished their work on the island. This is the kind of business I like to work up, and particularly so at this time of year."

Following the stock market crash of October, 1929, filming on Catalina continued unabated. The nation's crumbling economy didn't seem to affect movie goers—at first. The full impact of the Great Depression on the motion picture industry was still a year away. In the spring of 1930, Renton happily reported, "The movie business is picking up again at the Isthmus." Paramount scheduled a "million dollar picture" with a crew of 350 [*The Sea God*, starring Richard Arlen and Fay Wray]. The director told Renton that Catalina was the only place that they could make the film. Tiffany Studio booked the Isthmus for April [probably for *Aloha*, released in 1931] and Columbia for early May.

Renton found he could zip down to the Isthmus in twenty minutes on one of the *Miss Catalina* speedboats. He was kept busy juggling schedules for the various movie companies. "After having a wonderful April and such great crowds," he reported to Wrigley, "this week seemed dead on account of the rain. I was somewhat disappointed as I had Columbia Pictures Corporation coming over tomorrow to the Isthmus [to film *Hell's Island*], Paramount coming to Avalon, and also on the 12th a big Paramount company coming to the Isthmus. We have to make considerable changes up there to take care of the big group. We are putting up tents and getting everything ready, and our opening day of the season is not very far off.

"The manager [of Paramount] was over Saturday and claimed that his advance men would be down on the 15th and I hope it is true. However, you can never plan anything definite with the 'movies.' Putting electric heaters in the Banning House and Barracks and grading up all the streets and the old place looks like a real summer resort."

Filming at the Isthmus got so busy it was becoming like a Hollywood back lot. Sets were built, dismantled, rebuilt in new configurations. Studio personnel by the hundreds kept the dining hall and staff working full time. Renton, busy with other projects for Wrigley, hired a manager for the Isthmus facility. "I have a good man lined up for the whole proposition," he wrote. "He has worked at the Hotel St. Catherine [as storekeeper] for a number of years and knows how to watch the store. [Also] I will use Art LaShelle when the movie companies are actually on the ground since he understands their language. That makes a good combination."

A curious footnote to Tom White's involvement with Catalina is the movie *Sea Fury*, a melodramatic shipwreck, smuggling and mutiny picture made in 1929. It was filmed in part on the island and produced by Tom White. Despite White's enthusiasm for talking pictures, *Sea Fury* was a silent film, one of the last. Sound was added as an afterthought.

Paramount, for their ambitious picture *The Sea God*, needed sets at the Isthmus and at Johnson's and Howland's Landings. In late May, 1930, Renton drove the advance crews around to the locations before the carpenters with a barge load of materials arrived from the mainland. "Yesterday," he said, "was the first time I ever drove from Johnson's to Howland's and it was quite an adventure. The road is in fine shape except four or five places where there was only about two inches of space left outside of the wheels, but I got through all right. We are doing some work on this road so the 'movies' can transport their materials without going over the bank.

"They have one set at the Isthmus and another at Cherry Valley. [One] set at 4th of July Harbor representing a big jungle is one of the largest movie sets ever built on the island—forty feet high and one hundred and sixty feet long. In addition they have four or five barge loads of shrubbery in there, besides all the fake palm trees.

"The old Isthmus seems to be the busiest place on Catalina. Between the stars, cooks, actors, everything is going fine. The 'movies' are a temperamental bunch. They have great appetites. They have had two barges tied up to an anchor for the last three days, and a barge coming in every morning with shrubbery, trees, and 'junk' of all kinds. They are using our electric power, and it was necessary to make a rush job of moving two of our 2300-volt transformers from White's Landing to furnish enough power for their night work. They are going to have seventy-five mechanics come in; fifty others were supposed to come in three days later, and 300 actors. To feed this crowd alone means quite a great amount of study. We have filled up the Banning House, including the garage; the old Reinhart house (twelve cameramen in there), the old Tom White residence; all the various shacks and the barracks, and found it essential to erect one hundred tents in addition to those already in place. Of course, beds and mattresses that Tom White had available are not very comfortable, but the saying is that men in the picture business do not have to sleep very much—the main thing is to fill up their stomachs.

"We found it necessary to install new sinks in the kitchen, and also build some showers overnight to take care of 150 actors who were over-painted [with body paint].

Since the cold water would not remove the paint and give them proper baths, we installed a couple of electric water heaters. We had this stuff ordered one day and the next night we had cement floors, cement walls, and sufficient showers to take care of ten to fifteen at one time.

"You will recall I mentioned to you about our well at Howland's Landing running short of water for supplying the Isthmus. I ran the well rig up there and we sunk down eight to ten feet further and now seem to have plenty of water.

"On the way down I am going to have a hole drilled in Cherry Valley since that is a pretty big canyon, and should develop some more water for the Isthmus, which no doubt we will need. Also had a salt water line installed since thirty-five toilets take a lot of that water, and pumping from Howlands' Landing is a long way."

Wrigley was pleased with all the activity. He wrote, "Your movie business is like finding money. The Isthmus town is all yours. I bought it from Tom White and made it a present to the Santa Catalina Island Company. I am quite interested in what is going to happen there this summer."

By summer of 1930, Renton had his plans in place for expanding the tourist trade to the Isthmus. He wrote to Wrigley in June, "Discovered that a good number of the people going down to the Isthmus via bus are St. Catherine Hotel guests. Have made arrangements through the hotel that we would furnish these guests with luncheon at the Isthmus. If we get five cars full of people that means thirty-five people at $3.00, very good business. The last bunch of the 'movies' left the day before yesterday. We are going to send them an invoice complete which should show very close to $25,000 plus whatever the tug boats and barges take in.

"We are having a little opening at the Isthmus this Saturday. The old stage coach that belonged to the Bannings will be present and we are marking on the back of it with yellow letters '1884-1930.' The idea of this is to use the automobile to haul [visitors] one way and bring them back on the stage charging fifty cents apiece. This should make a 'hit' as a great many of the younger generation have never ridden in a [stage] coach.

"Holding the [steamer] *Cabrillo* at the Isthmus for an hour as we do at present on its trip from Wilmington is working out fine since it gives the passengers a chance to go into the restaurant and get some coffee and sandwiches, and since we have the best French pastry cook in the country, they seem to like this type of goods.

"I am arranging for a regular prop house [at the Isthmus]. It is surprising the amount of money you can get from old junk that is absolutely no good for anything else.

"As I told you, your friend [actor] Bill Farnum just put over a big 'talkie' and went over the top. He expects to make one of his pictures over here. Since he hadn't been over here for two years, he was astounded with what has been done, and the Casino certainly has him gasping. The best theater he had seen in the whole world."

Western star William Farnum, brother of Dustin Farnum, was an old Catalina hand. In the summer of 1920 he came to the island with a Fox Film Corporation crew to make *Drag Harlan*, a five-reel silent oater. The film was shot at Middle Ranch and involved bandit gangs, a lost gold mine, and a shoot out with the villains. Bill Farnum, when not before the camera, reported the *Catalina Islander*, was out fishing for tuna and swordfish. He later owned a home in Avalon.

In July, the movie concession was busier than ever. Renton wrote, "We have about one hundred guests down there in addition to the 'movies.' Fox Company expects to be there until the 10th [for *Seas Beneath*] and the Paramount troupe are expected to come back for another picture on the 13th [probably scenes for *Derelict*]. If we can get enough of this 'movie' business it will be gratifying. One hundred and eighty five passengers went to the Isthmus today on the *Cabrillo*, *Blanche W*, and *Betty O*. "

Later in the month he wrote, "We installed a dandy little golf course at the Isthmus in one week. Tonight we will have the lights set and be all ready to open up tomorrow. We have 130 'movies' there and we are preparing dinner for 300 to 350 persons for tomorrow night—the Commodores Cruise—involving all the yacht clubs around this section. Yesterday there was more activity down there [at the Isthmus] than in Hollywood. The 'movies' had two big [fresh water] tankers alongside the pier, as well as from fourteen to eighteen yachts."

While business at the Isthmus boomed, Avalon was beginning to feel the effects of the depression. Wrigley wrote, "The Isthmus seems to be doing very nicely—practically doing a marvelous business. This would be splendid if we would get an increase in business at Avalon. Of course, the extra business we get at the Isthmus helps make up the slump at Avalon. Everything is being run in the usual bang-up fashion.

"Every business throughout the United States, in fact, the world, is suffering a decrease over the boom year of 1929. I am extremely well pleased with the showing of everything we have at Avalon, which is doing very well in comparison to the wave of [bad] economy that is passing through [affecting] our customers.

"Note you are making a hundred percent clean-up of the Isthmus management; that shows me that the fellows were not up to date in attending to business. The Isthmus being so far away from your office [in Avalon], the gentlemen probably thought it wasn't necessary to do so much work. They will find out, however, that your eagle eye can see even twenty-five miles."

Wrigley was aware of changes in the movie industry wrought by the depression. Renton as well was aware of change in the air. As movie companies completed their work on Catalina, he saw few new projects to fill the gap. "The Isthmus," he wrote, "is not filled the way I would like to see it. This morning I have an appointment to go down there and meet one of the directors of Warner Brothers who is contemplating shooting a picture there. I want to get that business.

"We have had one movie company for a week. Also this week we expect to have the RKO outfit over [with] 100 to 125. The movie people are very hard to take care of, being very temperamental, and sometimes we feel like throwing them into the ocean. The amount of real cash money that we get from them, especially on the tugboat business and barges helps to cut down expenses of the rock business (Graham Brothers). Understand from Conner they got $1,800 from an old barge that was used in the production of a battleship, with tin guns mounted on 2x3's. These guns were twenty-five feet long and they sent them up to me for the prop pile. Of course, we will have to wait until we can catch another picture of this type to rent the guns."

At the end of September, 1930, Renton closed down the Isthmus facility, leaving only a skeleton crew, a watchman and one cook. In October, however, Fox arrived with a full crew [for John Ford's *Seas Beneath*].

"The Fox Company," Renton wrote, "is going to put in a big Spanish village. I bid on the lumber, but did not get it so I am letting them buy their own lumber and charging the usual rate for the tugboat business. The market for all commodities these days is so low and everyone is so hungry for business that they do not pay any attention at all to costs. Before the Fox Company gets their lumber delivered on the dock at the Isthmus, however, I know it will cost them more than if we quoted them f.o.b. Isthmus, but that is their business. "

The Fox picture was a bright light in an otherwise gloomy fall on the island. Renton wrote, "We are very fortunate to have Fox down here. In fact we are doing more business at the Isthmus than all of our hotels and villas [in Avalon] put together. The 'movies' have in the neighborhood of one hundred or more and expect to bring in another hundred on Saturday. We have the barracks, Banning House and all the other houses filled and, of course, quite a few of the tents. At the present time we have plenty of blankets at Avalon not being used, which we can send down to the Isthmus."

The following spring, Renton readied the Isthmus facility, but he sounded less than optimistic. "Am trying to get the Isthmus opened up," he wrote. "Imagine one of these days we will get a call for a movie location."

A few days later, after a call came in, Renton was his usual enthusiastic self. "Am going to the Isthmus tomorrow to get everything lined up there. The road is in A-1 shape. I drove a movie outfit down there a few days ago. I sold them [on] a location and expect to have from 100 to 125 people in about three weeks time for eight to fifteen days. That's providing, of course, nothing happens to the movies. We also expect to have the Paramount outfit this weekend for one night only at the St. Catherine. They will have about one hundred in their party."

After his return to Avalon, Renton wrote, "By the end of the week, we will have twenty-five [new] bungalettes about completed. In another week we expect to formally open the Isthmus. We will feature it in publicity and bring down the Mexican Mariachi Band. We will have pretty señoritas taking part in the festivities. By featuring excellent seafood at the Isthmus, we will attract many people coming to Avalon in search of a real 'shore dinner.' The chef at the Isthmus is quite skilled. Even though this is a year of depression, it looks like our business will equal if not exceed last year's business."

The following month Renton reported that the Isthmus opening went over with a bang, with over twelve hundred people present. In the afternoon, a Pathé film crew arrived to shoot background scenes. "After July 4th we have promise of a United Artists location company of 125 or more for about a three-week stay [for *Corsair*, with Chester Morris].The producers are not throwing much money away at the present time. They are watching their hours pretty closely and making the actors and other men work instead of loafing most of the day."

Renton kept close watch on the movie facility during the summer of 1931, knowing how important film making was to the overall economy of Catalina. He reported to Wrigley, "The place is running entirely to my pleasure, and I have a very good man as manager. The 'movies' inconvenience the kitchen and dining room crews sometimes by ordering dinner for 12:00 noon and not showing up until 3:00 PM. However, I have a few extra hands to help and everything runs smoothly enough. The past week they have been working nights as well as days on their picture. By keeping everything open until early morning, we take in considerable revenues.

"The old set that Paramount left at the Isthmus last year has been fixed up with a floor and washbasin and toilet. It was left in the same colorful, crude and rustic state and we rented it for $175 for the month to a group of yachtsmen. Everyone demands the new bungalettes, especially with the toilets and washbasins. As you know, instead of building fifty, I built only twenty-five. The old 'Sadie Thompson' house on the avenue just beyond the dining room is being made into a three-room unit. As you remember, the porch runs the entire length of the front as well as on the sides. The inside has been finished off with Celotex, but the outside has been left as it was in the movies. The place will be known as the 'Sadie Thompson Set' and will have a lot of publicity value. The little improvements to these sets will not cost much, but will give the movie flavor to the Isthmus, which people seem to enjoy."

Renton continued to merge movie company needs with visitor amenities at the Isthmus. Somehow he managed to keep one group from getting in the other's way. After all, one of the main reasons the movies companies liked to use Catalina for location shooting was the lack of crowds. That summer at the Isthmus, United Artists did return to film *Corsair*, a "rum-running picture," as Renton described it, using Catalina Island Company trucks and the Wilmington Transportation Company's barges and tugs.

Renton wrote, "You can imagine the way the Isthmus has been looking—like a movie shack town with actors and 'extras' and millionaires of all description—some living in the bungalettes and others on yachts. The food has been good and everyone likes to swim. Today I am ordering some more fishing tackle for the store at the Isthmus as we practically sold out all we had.

"The old shack that stood at the entrance to the dock has been changed into what might represent a movie set and we will use it as a shop. Half of it will be a Chinese shop and the other half will be Spanish. I am going to have a girl dressed in oriental costume on the Chinese side and a fellow dressed in typical Spanish costume on the other. We will have the Mexican Band at the restaurant/fountain, which should stir things up."

"The 'Sadie Thompson' house made a hit with everyone who saw it. It is very unique and is now rented. The old movie set at the entrance to the pier has been fixed up for a [Catalina] pottery display, and also has a Chinese display featuring the old [Chinese junk] *Ning Po*. The old hulk of the *Ning Po* in Catalina Harbor fell apart last week."

Wrigley wrote to Renton in August, "There is absolutely no doubt about it, the fact that we have been financially able to take care of our property during this long and continuous slump, and we have kept everything up to date and given our visitors a little more for their money—and a lively, clean healthy place—is one of the reasons why our business has fallen down so little in comparison to that of other resorts.

"I imagine you and Phil will some of these days get a great kick out of building up the Isthmus and trying to make it a larger city even than Avalon. We will, however, have to wait until people have money to spend before we can do that."

William Wrigley, Jr. didn't live to see the transformation at the Isthmus. He died January 26, 1932, age seventy, at his home in Phoenix. David Renton continued to correspond with Wrigley's wife Ada, and J. H. Patrick, president of the Santa Catalina Island Company. By July, 1932, Renton reported to thirty-eight-year-old Philip K. Wrigley, the new president of the Company.

During this time, a United Artists film crew of 178 occupied the Isthmus for the production of *Rain*, starring Joan Crawford. Renton reported that he had to settle some squabbles between the "movies." "I went down to the Isthmus last Friday. There are two movie companies there at the present time, Warner Brothers and United Artists. They seem to be having a bit of trouble with a group of about eight people who were trying to cause trouble with Joan Crawford's hairdresser and with several laborers. The movie outfits were very much upset, as they did not think they would be troubled at Catalina. I asked them if they wanted me to try and straighten things out, so I went up to the leader of the group and tapped him on the shoulder, led him down to the dock, and put him on the boat. I told him that he was on private property, and if he ever set foot there again, we would lock him up for the night. The men went back to work, and the motion picture people seemed very pleased, and that was that.

"The Fox Company got in on Friday. They are building a set in front of the dining

room for a picture they are making called *After the Rain* [*The Painted Woman*]. They sent one of our large barges full of equipment. The whole Isthmus looks busy. I am having some pictures taken, and I am going to send some back so that you and Phil can see them. Lewis Milestone, the director, has been hard to handle but I have acquired a lot of patience handling picture people all these years.

"Fox called up and wants to make a picture [*The Golden West*] in the interior of the island using our buffalo as background. It is pretty hard trading these times, even with the 'movies,' but I will try to work out the best possible arrangement."

A letter from Renton to Patrick a few days later reveals how the movie business on Catalina remained relatively active even as California and the nation sank deeper into the depression. "A company from Warner Brothers has been here for about ten days, and we expect a party from MGM the latter part of the week [for scenes in *Fast Life*]. A director from Paramount was here yesterday looking for a location. They plan to be here the latter part of the month. Warner Brothers has one tug and a barge that they have been using along with nearly all our truck equipment. Part of them are staying at the St. Catherine and the rest at the Atwater."

Renton wrote to Philip Wrigley about branching out into western movies. "We now have the Fox Company taking a shot up at Empire Flats, this side of the Isthmus Summit [for *The Golden West*]. They brought over six horses. George O'Brien is the star rider. We sold them 15,000 feet of lumber for the corrals and chutes to run the buffalo in. There are thirty-five in the group staying at the Isthmus. They have three cars and three trucks hired from us. Understand they will want about three of your horses from your ranch as well as the use of your cowboys. Your horses and men took in revenues [for work on the movie] which will be credited to your ranch. This is not so bad for our first start on western pictures.

"Last week I was coming home from the Isthmus with Harry Gribbon, the film comedian, and as he wanted to take the boat, I talked him into riding with me [in my car.] He certainly was one scared movie star. We had two other movie people in the back seat, and Gribbon wanted to know if they would excuse him while he took a drink, as he was so scared. I kept the car very close to the bank and tried to talk to him to get his mind off the height and the curves. By the time we got to Avalon he was pretty near a wreck. He said I was a very good mountain driver, which pleased me very much."

Patrick wrote back, "I note you arrived over the mountain with Mr. Harry Gribbon and have no doubt that if you pointed out the scenery with both hands while going around the curves it might be destructive to his nerves. Have had the same feeling many times myself but I notice you always arrive safely."

Warner Brothers arrived on Catalina with a crew of hundreds in September 1932, to make a comedy around the 1927 Catalina Ocean Marathon. That contest, sponsored by William Wrigley, Jr., saw over one hundred intrepid swimmers enter the water at Isthmus Cove and make for the mainland twenty-two miles away. Fifteen hours and forty-six minutes later, one swimmer emerged to claim the prize money and become the first known swimmer of the Catalina Channel. The event received nationwide publicity. Renton wrote to Philip Wrigley, "Warner Brothers will probably remain here all this week. They are shooting the Catalina Swim, using Joe E. Brown and Ginger Rogers, the little redhead co-star. The name of the picture is *You Said a Mouthful!* We are in hopes to have MGM over the latter part of this week or next week. The 'movies' are very much like swallows—if one makes a picture in a certain place, they all want to follow.

"Hauled 750 Warner Brothers 'movies' to the Isthmus [from Avalon] where we had to set up a barbeque for them. We only had one day's notice, which was quite a task. The night before, after we had all the tables set up, the 'movies' decided they were in the wrong location and would be in the way of their shooting. So we had to move the whole layout. This rather upsets the men who work hard to get everything prepared. Of Course, the 'movies' will pay for the change. We also had about 200 [guests] from Avalon. The dining room served 400 people, the fountain did a tremendous business, and the whole affair was a very profitable day.

"Warner Brothers publicity men wanted us to put on a prize dance at the Casino [in Avalon] Saturday night so their stars could act as judges. We put on a prize waltz and they had Joe E. Brown, [director] Lloyd Bacon, and a few of their officials act as judges. We had some very good dancers and everybody enjoyed the event. The 'movies' had their cameraman shoot pictures of the affair, which they will use for publicity. They had their own star, Ginger Rogers come out on the floor, but she did not look very graceful after seeing the other prize winners. There are very few movie stars that look good after they get their makeup off."

Philip Wrigley noted, "You are certainly keeping the movie business going at the

Isthmus. They not only want to use the same locations but apparently all want to make exactly the same kind of pictures at the same time—they are all either aviation pictures, all wild animal pictures, or all travel pictures."

In October, Renton wrote of a stroke of luck. "We had a chance to get a bull buffalo, two cows and three calves, and one elk delivered to our dock at Wilmington from the County [of Los Angeles] for free. I thought this might make a good mixture with the buffalo we have at the present time. Don't think we could get them any cheaper. My idea to get additional buffalo is use them possibly for future movie companies. Also had a chance to get three or four bears, but I did not think it advisable to take them."

Philip Wrigley responded, "Think it is an excellent idea to get a little new blood added to our buffalo herd. As you know, I have been trying to get some buffalo for a year or so, but they have all been at fancy prices. We certainly cannot get stuck on getting something for nothing. I agree with you that the bears might not be good, even if they were tame. Doubt if I would want to meet one in a lonely spot on the Island, especially with our scarcity of trees to climb."

That same month as the rains began on Catalina, Paramount was finishing a picture at the Isthmus. Renton reported, "The other night we had lots of excitement down there with some intoxicated yachtsmen. It's a wonder that someone did not get killed as the movie extras were all wrestlers and prizefighters being used as half-men,-half monkey characters in the play *The Island of Lost Men* [*Island of Lost Souls*]. You certainly would have gotten a laugh out of it if you had been there. One of the [drunk] yachtsmen grabbed the vest of a 'Turk' who can lift 250 pounds over his head without any trouble and is supposed to be the strongest man in the world. The yachtsman ripped the whole front of [the 'Turk's] vest off, which contained the 'Turk's watch. Being of slow thought, all the 'Turk' could think of was his watch. If he had gotten mad, the director was afraid someone would have been killed. We [will] make an example of these yachtsmen for interfering with the 'movies.' We have a warrant out for their arrest with $1,000 bail."

MGM was filming in Avalon [for *Fast Life*], using about a hundred residents as extras at $5.00 per day each. Renton reported, "We still have MGM in Avalon waiting for the weather to clear. I went down to the Isthmus yesterday, as Paramount was leaving. It was certainly some mud-hole. The rain came down in bucketfuls. We have another independent company coming in Wednesday."

The movie facility shut down for the winter after that. However, in February, 1933, Warner Brothers expressed an interest in filming a new movie off season. "[They] sent a party over yesterday," Renton wrote, "to look at locations at Catalina Harbor where they expect to make a sea picture. They expect to be there a week or more, and we told them we would have to make a charge for opening up the Isthmus [facilities]. I am making arrangement to cut down on board and room to conform to prices on the other side [mainland]. We do not charge movie people for locations on which to shoot their pictures, something which they have to pay in other places, and there is no better location than the Isthmus for the type of picture they are making."

Warner Brothers began work shortly after. "They had wonderful weather while they were building their sets and now they are ready to shoot. We made them as comfortable as possible, and had to bring in a couple of coal stoves to heat the dining room.

"We arranged with various location managers to have their cameramen come over and take a number of pictures of different places on the Island which might be used as locations in filming of future pictures. These pictures will be kept on file, and whenever they need a location, they can refer to them.

"The picture they [Warner Brothers] are making is *Narrow Corners* [*The Narrow Corner*], and the scenes are supposed to be laid in Java. Most of the scenes are being shot on the Catalina Harbor side where the old boats are, but some are being taken on the Isthmus side. Douglas Fairbanks, Jr. is one of the stars, with a very fine chap by the name of [Alfred E.] Green directing. Green is one of our very good guests at the Hotel St. Catherine."

In 1933 RKO Radio Pictures released *King Kong* and it became an instantaneous box office smash. The studio immediately began work on a sequel and many exterior scenes were shot on Catalina.

That summer, a strike in Hollywood curtailed much of the movie making business. And Renton made no mention of it until February, 1934. He wrote to Mrs. William Wrigley, Jr., "The Paramount people are planning to come over the 15th of this month for four or five days [probably to shoot underwater scenes for *No More Women*, a Victor McLaglen, Edmund Lowe comedy]. There will be sixty people in the group and they will stay at the Atwater and the St. Catherine hotels. There are at least three stories that will start in production within the next month or so which look very promising for the

Isthmus location. Art La Shelle is keeping in close touch with the studios to get them to come to the Island."

Art La Shelle was, at that time, manager of the Isthmus movie-making facility. Renton divided the Isthmus business into the resort operations and the motion picture locations operations. Both operations shared many of the same facilities, depending on demand, such as the barracks, bungalettes, tents, houses and offices, and dining room.

Two big movies were made on Catalina in the spring of 1934. One was *We're Not Dressing*, Paramount's musical comedy remake of the 1919 movie *Male and Female*. The plot was set on a yacht owned by a fabulously rich heiress. The yacht is wrecked on a deserted island, and fun and games ensue. Bing Crosby, Carole Lombard, Burns and Allen, Ethyl Merman and Leon Errol led the cast. Most scenes were shot at White's Landing, near Avalon, where cast and crew stayed for the production.

The other big movie was MGM's *Treasure Island*, with Wallace Beery, Jackie Cooper, Otto Kruger and Lionel Barrymore. Originally scheduled for location work near Honolulu, the movie relocated to Catalina, the choice of director Victor Fleming. In April, Renton wrote to Philip K. Wrigley, "The construction men for MGM are at [Johnson's Landing] building sets. The men intend to be here about one week on this job and the troupe of about eighty is expected to arrive about Monday of next week [and] probably stay here around two or three weeks."

Two weeks later, he wrote, "MGM expects to complete their work next Wednesday unless they are delayed by Wallace Beery, whose wife is seriously ill. He has been using the seaplane every day, [flying to Los Angeles and] spending the night with her."

Thereafter, Renton reported weekly on the picture's progress. "The 'movies' are changing the location of their sets over to Catalina Harbor and will be back for five or six days. Before they finish this picture we should get in the neighborhood of $20,000 from them.

"The sea unit of *Treasure Island* returned on Saturday, seven in number. The construction crew came in yesterday and the main troupe will come in Thursday. This will last only a couple of days which will complete the picture."

"The *Treasure Island* clean-up crew left Emerald Bay and the Isthmus in good condition." And finally, "MGM has entirely completed *Treasure Island* and we are expecting more business from them in the near future as they have one or two stories coming up

which are quite apt to be filmed on the Isthmus."

1935 was a big year for Catalina in the movies. In addition to the blockbuster *Mutiny on the Bounty* with Clark Gable, Catalina saw the filming of *Captain Blood* with Errol Flynn, *I Live My Life* with Joan Crawford and Brian Aherne, and *Murder on a Honeymoon* with Edna May Oliver and James Gleason. *Captain Blood* used no full-size ships in filming at sea, instead relying on process shots and miniatures. In addition First National used footage from the 1924 silent film *The Sea Hawk*, not to be confused with the 1924 version of *Captain Blood*. Both stories, by Rafael Sabatini, are similar. The sea battles for *The Sea Hawk* were filmed at Catalina Harbor and nearby Point Torquemada.

For the MGM production of *I Live My Life*, Catalina became the Greek Island of Naxos, where archeologist Brian Aherne was working. Society girl Joan Crawford meets him and falls in love. After building a set on the hills above Isthmus Cove replicating Greek ruins, the film was delayed a month due to fog, a Catalina rarity in the summer.

Murder on a Honeymoon, RKO's detective comedy, is set in Avalon and includes wonderful footage of the Bird Park, Casino, and the airport. Through this movie, many people around the country for the first time saw Catalina as it really looked.

During the depression years, movie goers enjoyed light comedies and flashy musicals, escapes from harsher realities. Paramount returned to Catalina in 1936 to shoot parts of the musical comedy *The Big Broadcast of 1936*. Along with many other performers, some from *We're Not Dressing* returned too, Bing Crosby, Burns and Allen and Ethyl Merman. This time Catalina Island became the fictitious island kingdom of Clemente, a name play on neighboring San Clemente Island. That same year David M. Renton retired, leaving the movie-making facility at the Isthmus in the capable hands of Art La Shelle.

Other films that include Catalina scenes made in the late 1930s reflect the continuing popularity of South Sea island adventures and sea stories. These include *Isle of Fury* with Humphrey Bogart, *Ebb Tide* with Frances Farmer and Ray Milland, *The Hurricane* with Dorothy Lamour and John Hall, *Souls at Sea* with Gary Cooper and George Raft, *The Buccaneer* with Frederick March, *Rulers of the Sea* with Douglas Fairbanks, Jr., *Slave Ship* with Warner Baxter, Wallace Beery and Mickey Rooney, and *Captain Calamity* with George Houston and Marian Nixon.

Captain Calamity, with outdoor scenes shot at the Isthmus, was made by Regal Productions in two versions, English and Spanish, shot simultaneously using different actors in each. Starring in the Spanish version were Bona Nova and Movita Castaneda, who played opposite Clark Gable in *Mutiny on the Bounty*.

The Hurricane, made by Samuel Goldwyn in 1937, contained the ultimate "South Seas" special effects, a full-blown hurricane. The plan was to film the entire picture in the South Seas but the cost proved prohibitive. Most of the background footage, however, was shot in Pago Pago, American Samoa. Other background shots were made on Catalina Island. Ironically, another concern over shooting entirely in the South Seas was the possibility of bad weather. The hurricane itself was staged on a two-and-a-half acre United Artists backlot in Hollywood. A full-scale native village, built for $125,000, was destroyed by the special effects crew for another $250,000. A Catalina footnote to this movie, one of the Tahitian dancers brought to the Island for the picture fell in love with one of the cameramen, married, and the couple lived thereafter in Avalon.

Movie studios by the late 1930s appreciated the publicity value of exotic foreign locations. Typically, a studio would announce the foreign location and downplay the Catalina and backlot scenes. Twentieth Century Fox, for *Slave Ship* in 1937, sent one crew to Bermuda and another to Catalina. The sea scenes were intermixed to create the impression that the movie was shot entirely on and around Bermuda.

War in Europe and the Far East in 1940 foreclosed many foreign locations. Catalina Island, however, continued to stand in for the South Seas. In background shots for *The Road to Singapore* with Bing Crosby, Bob Hope and Dorothy Lamour, Catalina becomes the fictional island kingdom of Kaigoon.

When America entered World War II in December, 1941, life on Catalina Island abruptly changed. Restrictions on pleasure boating along the West Coast kept yachtsmen from the island and the Navy and Coast Guard even "requisitioned" certain private yachts for wartime use. The steamers *Catalina* and *Avalon* became troop ferries stationed in San Francisco Bay for the duration. Early in 1942, following isolated attacks on the California coast by Japanese submarines, the waters off Catalina were viewed as a potential hiding place for enemy submarines waiting to attack ships departing Los Angeles Harbor. The tourist trade ended and many of Catalina's young men went off to war or to work on the mainland in defense industries. The island was not deserted however, for the U.S. Maritime Service turned Avalon into a training base, occupying hotels, homes, and even the Casino. Big bands and movie stars continued to appear in the theater and ballroom to entertain the troops. Coast guard recruits, sent to Catalina for training, were housed at the Isthmus in the movie company facilities.

Photography by civilians, both movies and still photographs was forbidden at all coastal facilities including Catalina Island. Commercial movie making on Catalina came to a halt. Yachting scenes for Twentieth Century Fox's romantic comedy *Rings on Her*

Fingers, shot in January 1942, were the last "civilian" scenes set on Catalina until the summer of 1945. The war film *Guadalcanal Diary*, made in 1943 under close scrutiny by military advisors, was shot primarily at Camp Pendleton, the big Marine training base near Oceanside, California. Some scenes were shot under close scrutiny on Catalina at Little Harbor. Training films made for the military in 1944 include brief shots of Catalina facilities. By the summer of 1945, the threat of Japanese submarines or sabotage had ended. Movie companies eased out of wartime restrictions on outdoor coastal photography. MGM came to Catalina to film outdoor scenes near the Casino and Seal Rocks for *Adventure*, starring Clark Gable.

After the war, Catalina welcomed back the movie companies. Other locations, however, competed with Catalina for movie business and fewer films were shot on the island during the post-war years. Visitors, however, returned in large numbers, boating, fishing, and recreational diving resumed. Avalon and the Isthmus once again became popular destinations for movie stars eager to escape the rigors of Hollywood.

In 1947, the film-making facilities at the Isthmus underwent an overhaul to accommodate filming a fifteen-part serial *The Sea Hounds*, starring Buster Crabbe. The *Catalina Islander* reported in the May 15th issue that a new kitchen was installed for the dining hall, and the bungalows were renovated. The movie company, Esskay Productions, headed by David and Sam Katzman, consisted of 125 people, who stayed for a month. They brought two barge loads of equipment and special sets, including a sailing ship interior. David Renton's old "Sadie Thompson" house left over from the 1928 Gloria Swanson movie became a South Seas trading post for *The Sea Hounds*.

In the early 1950s, the Hollywood movie industry faced a greater threat to its existence than that posed by the great depression. Televison. What had started as a novelty with blurry little black and white images, had quickly developed into an entertainment colossus. In an ironic twist, vaudeville acts of the 1920s, put out of work by the advent of "talking" movies, found a new home on televison. After sound movies had eliminated the need for opening live acts, or prologues, vaudeville performers, those who could, made the transition to radio. A few, such as Bob Hope, Jack Benny, Jimmy Durante and Burns and Allen had survived to become big radio stars and had film careers as well. But television's small screen was a natural home for comedians and actors who needed little more than a stage and a live audience.

Hollywood felt television's impact at the box office. People stayed home in droves to watch Milton Berle or even old movies, all free of charge. Even performers who had started in the movies, such as Red Skelton, Lucille Ball and Dinah Shore, moved to television. The big studios responded by making bigger, more spectacular movies that television couldn't match. Major studio productions in wide screen format often relied on distant romantic locations to lure audiences. That meant Catalina as a stand in for more glamorous spots was relegated to "B" movies or low-budget independent productions. But what Catalina lost in major movie work, it gained in television films. And television shows needed commercials to sell sponsor's products. Television commercials evolved from simple announcements to carefully choreographed and photographed short films. Competition for the viewer's attention often meant filming outside the studio. Catalina, once more, became a popular venue for film making, this time for television shows, documentaries and commercials.

One of the first TV films shot on Catalina was *Nocturne*, in 1949. In 1950 several film segments were shot for TV shows including *Hollywood on the Line*, *Magazine on the Air*, and *For Sportsmen Only*. In the early 1950s Catalina became the location for episodes of *Queen for a Day*, *Truth or Consequences*, *You Asked For It*, and the *Lawrence Welk Show*. Starting in 1958, *Sea Hunt*, starring Lloyd Bridges, regularly filmed underwater scenes at White's Landing. Other TV shows that managed to film at least one episode on Catalina include *Route 66*, *McHale's Navy*, *The Persuaders*, *Malibu Run*, *Cannon*, *Barnaby Jones*, *Mannix*, *Emergency*, *Code R*, *The Dating Game*, *Power Rangers*, *Baywatch*, *The Love Boat*, and *Murder She Wrote*. Even the soaps, such as *Days of Our Lives*, have set episodes on Catalina. Television sports shows featuring Catalina include *MTV Skyjumpers*, *Catalina Xtreme Golf*, *Inline Hockey News*, *Fox Sports*, and many sailing, fishing and scuba diving films.

Televison commercials shot on Catalina are too numerous to list. The island's photogenic features that delight film makers work as well in commercials as in feature movies. From the mid-1950s film crews producing television commercials have been familiar sights on Catalina. Clients over the years have ranged from Coca Cola and Toyota to Victoria's Secret. Fashion photography and other advertising "still" shoots are common on Catalina as well. In recent years Catalina has provided the backdrop for music videos and cable televison channels such as Tech TV, the Travel Channel, Christian Network TV, The Learning Channel, and PBS.

As everybody knows, Hollywood did not succumb to television. It absorbed it. Big studios bought or merged with television production companies, others started their own. New York based corporations ended up owning and controlling both movie and television production, as well as broadcasting networks and chains of movie theaters. But that is another story. For feature film makers, Catalina Island continued its allure.

Underwater photography, featured in films from the late 1940s onward, was perfect for Catalina's spectacular undersea gardens. Better cameras and advances in self-contained underwater breathing apparatus, or "scuba "gear, a wartime development, meant underwater cameramen could follow the action as never before. Island resident and expert diver Al Hansen shot underwater scenes for such movies as *Monster From the Ocean Floor*, 1954, and *The Phantom From 10,000 Leagues*, the following year. Other films with underwater scenes include *Wake of the Red Witch* starring John Wayne, *Jupiter's Darling* with Esther Williams, *Ghost Diver* in 1957, and *Atlantis, The Lost Continent*, filmed in 1960. Even Elvis got into the scuba act in the 1967 musical comedy *Easy Come, Easy Go.* The year before, Catalina Island got to play a feature role in the Doris Day comedy *The Glass Bottom Boat*. Perhaps the best known underwater scenes in movies are those in *Jaws* and *Jaws II* Both films incorporated shots made on, or under, Catalina.

An attribute of Catalina popular with movie makers over the years is its isolated coves and beaches. With a little creative camera work, they can become romantic, desolate, or even sinister. In the 1968 horror classic *Rosemary's Baby*, set in New York City, Mia Farrow's character, Rosemary, endures a dream sequence filmed at Catalina's Little Harbor and Shark Harbor. In countless films, pirates have waded ashore on deserted islands or marooned their victims on bleak, windswept beaches, all on Catalina just a few miles along the coast from Avalon.

Another film classic incorporating Catalina footage is Roman Polanski's *Chinatown*. This 1974 atmospheric mystery set in 1930s Los Angeles, stars Jack Nickolson, Fay Dunaway and John Huston. In the story Huston's character, an evil rich old man, owns the "Albacore Club," where private eye Nickolson confronts him. The scene was shot at Avalon with the Tuna Club posing as the Albacore Club.

In Universal's 1977 production of *MacArthur*, starring Gregory Peck, the Catalina Isthmus once again stands in for a South Seas locale. In this instance it is Corregidor, the island fortress in the Philippines where, in 1942, Douglas MacArthur was forced to escape the oncoming Japanese army. In recent years, Catalina Island has had numerous cameo roles in the movies, often in the form of "pick up" shots used as transitions between scenes or augmentation to scenes shot elsewhere. Examples include *Waterworld, Dick Tracy*, *Armistad*, and *Pearl Harbor.*

Today the vast majority of Catalina is owned by the Santa Catalina Island Conservancy dedicated to preservation of the island's natural resources. The unique geography thus protected, plus the island's proximity to Hollywood, insures that film makers will continue to seek out Catalina's visual charms. The century-old tradition of Catalina "in the movies" will endure.

CATALINA IN THE MOVIES
Part 3: The List

From *The Black Pirate*, 1926

AUTHOR'S NOTE:

The following list, a work in progress, is compiled from several sources, primarily the American Film Institute Catalog, *The Catalina Islander*, and Avalon city records. Movies listed include major studio productions with all or most outdoor scenes filmed on Catalina, those with a few Catalina locale scenes, and those with occasional scenes or "pick up" shots made on or around the Island. I'm sure many more early one-reel shorts and comedies were filmed on Catalina but documentation and the films themselves have been lost. Other films not listed are some that include brief underwater, landscape or seascape scenes unrecognizable as Catalina Island. Not included are the hundreds of TV shows, commercials, educational, scientific and promotional films shot over the years. The movies are grouped by the year filmed, not necessarily the year released. Titles listed are release titles, not necessarily working titles.

1910

FEEDING SEALS AT CATALINA ISLE Essanay Film Mfg. Co. First known commercial movie made on Catalina. One reel, 170 feet, split with another movie, *Up-to-date Servants.*

1911

(WHALING FILM), no known title. Produced by Hobart Bosworth.

1912

MAN'S GENESIS Biograph. Dir. D. W. Griffith. May Marsh, Wilfred Lucas, Robert Harron. Incorporated into another film, *Primitive Man* in 1913.

1913

(NO NAME) Balboa Film Company.

CAVEMAN'S WAR Kalem.

PRIMITIVE MAN Kalem. Incorporated *Man's Genesis* from 1912.

THE SEA WOLF Bosworth, Inc. Dir. Hobart Bosworth. Cast: Hobart Bosworth, Herbert Rawlinson, Viola Barry, cameo by Jack London. First authorized movie of Jack London's classic story of cruelty at sea.

1914

THE DEAD LINE Nestor Film Company, released by Crosby Motion Picture Co. David Hartford.

A DAY AT CATALINA Keystone. Fatty Arbuckle. Probably a promo film for Catalina or a short subject.

CAPTAIN ALVAREZ Vitagraph: A Broadway Star Feature. Dir. Rollin S. Sturgeon. Edith Storey, William Desmond Taylor, George S. Holt. An American in Argentina falls in love, fights a despot, escapes from capture and is reunited with his lady.

NEPTUNE'S DAUGHTER Universal Film Co. Dir. Herbert Brenon. Annette Kellerman Katherine Lee, Herbert Brenon, William Welch. The mermaid daughter of Neptune seeks revenge against a fishing kingdom responsible for her sister's death in a fishing net. She assumes human form and instead of killing the king, falls in love with him. Shot in Bermuda with "pick up" scenes on Catalina. Unrelated to 1949 MGM film released with the same title

THE SEA NYMPHS Keystone. Prod. Mack Sennett and Fatty Arbuckle. Gloria Swanson, Old Ben, the seal.

SELIG Film Co. No recorded subject or title.

THE SMUGGLERS Biograph. Dir. Sidney Olcott. Donald Brian, Olive Tell, Cyril Chadwick. Fun and games and double cross between a man and his wife, an expensive necklace and a fake copy.

A SHIP WRECK Universal. May be working title, or footage used for another picture.

THE VALLEY OF THE MOON Bosworth. Dir. Hobart Bosworth. Jack Conway, Myrtle Stedman, Ernest Garcia, prologue by Jack London. One of the series of Jack London stories filmed by Bosworth, shot in San Francisco, Catalina, and Glen Ellen, London's ranch.

WHO'S WHO Universal. Split reel, Will Lewis.

ZODIAK Film Mfg. Co. Dir. James A. Crosby

1915

ADVENTURE OF A MADCAP Balboa Film Co. Filmed aboard boat *Nellie*.

NELL OF THE NOTIONS Lasky Feature Play Co.

OUT OF THE DARKNESS Lasky Feature Play Co./ Paramount. Dir. George Melford. Marjorie Daw, Hal Clements, Tom Forman, Loyola O'Conner. Socialite heiress with a yacht in Florida suffers amnesia and ends up working in her own cannery. Recovering her memory, she fights to improve working conditions.

A SUBMARINE PIRATE Keystone/Triangle. Sup. Mack Sennett. Dir. Sidney Chaplin. Glen Cavender, Wesley Ruggles, Phyllis Allen. Comedy starring Sid Chaplin (Charlie's brother), who devised many of the underwater shots of a submarine borrowed from the U.S. Navy.

THE WOMAN Lasky Feature Play Co./Paramount. Dir. George Melford. Theodore Roberts, James Neill, Ernest Joy. Drama. Crooked politicians try to smear a senator by planting a woman in his hotel room. The plan backfires. Avalon doubles for town in Maine.

YOUNG ROMANCE Lasky Feature Play Co. Cast includes Edith Taliaferro.

1916

THE BATTLE OF HEARTS Fox Film Corp. Dir. Oscar Apfel. William Farnum, Elda Furry, Wheeler Oakman. Drama. Lighthouse keeper shuts down light to aid his smuggling activity, but causes his girlfriend's sailboat to crash. Fishing fleet owner Farnum gets the girl.

CIVILIZATION Thomas H. Ince Productions. Dir. Thomas H. Ince, Raymond B. West, Reginald Barker. Cast: Herschel Mayall, Lola May, Howard Hickman, Enid Markey. Drama involving a submarine and a mythical kingdom. Film shot immediately after the 1915 Avalon fire were incorporated into the movie.

THE PEARL OF PARADISE Pollard Picture Play for Mutual. Dir. Harry Pollard. Margarita Fischer, Harry Pollard, Joseph Harris. Probably the first "South Sea Island" movie made on Catalina.

TO HAVE AND TO HOLD Lasky/Paramount. Director George H. Melford. Mae Murray, Wallace Reid, Tom Forman. Costume drama, set in colonial America. Gentleman and his bride-to-be end up on a pirate island (Catalina) escaping the clutches of an evil pursuer.

THE SEA NYMPHS Keystone Mutual. Prod. Mack Sennett. Mable Normand, Fatty Arbuckle .

UNDINE Bluebird Photoplays. Dir. Henry Otto. Ida Schnall, Douglas Gerrard, Edna Maison. Fantasy about Undine, most skillful water nymph in an undersea kingdom, who marries a mortal. Their daughter, also called Undine, must atone for her mother's transgression.

1917

DOWN TO EARTH (THE OPTIMIST) Douglas Fairbanks Pictures. Dir. John Emerson. Douglas Fairbanks, Eileen Percy. Comedy. Big game hunter rescues his lady friend and other inmates from a sanitarium and escapes on his yacht. Shipwreck on a desert island follows, where the inmates are rehabilitated.

STOWAWAYS AND STRATEGY Western Vitagraph. Dir. J.A. Howe. No record, may be working title.

WHEN A MAN SEES RED Fox Film Corp. Dir. Frank Lloyd. William Farnum, Jewel Carmen, G. Raymond Nye. Drama. A sailor ships out with his sister's murderer seeking revenge. He falls in love with a millionaire's mistress who is shipwrecked on a South Seas Island. Sailor rescues her and kills her captor, who also did in his sister.

1918

BRASS BULLET Universal. Dir. Ben Wilson. An 18-part serial. Episode Seven, *The Depth Bomb*, set on Catalina.

SWORDFISHING WITH ROD AND REEL AT CATALINA ISLAND Pyramid Film Co. Educational film.

CAMPING OUT Lasky/Paramount. Fatty Arbuckle. Two-reel comedy.

HUMDRUM BROWN Paralta Plays, Inc. Dir. Rex Ingram. Henry B. Walthall, Mary Charleson, Dorothy Love. Comedy-drama. Humdrum bank clerk works hard to save his bank after it is pilfered by crook. He captures the crook on board a steamer from San Francisco.

TREASURE ISLAND Fox Film Corp. Dir. C.M. Franklin and S.A. Franklin. Francis Carpenter, Virginia Corbin, Herschel Mayall, Elmo Lincoln. Classic story by Robert Louis Stevenson. Peg-leg pirate, squawking parrot, adventure, mutiny, and buried treasure.

1919

THE ISLAND OF INTRIGUE Metro Pictures, Inc. Dir. Henry Otto.

MALE AND FEMALE Famous Players-Lasky. Dir. Cecil B. DeMille. Thomas Meighan, Theodore Roberts, Raymond Hatton, Gloria Swanson, Bebe Daniels. Society drama. Rich man's yacht, loaded with family and servants, wrecks on South Sea island. The butler falls in love with yachtsman's daughter, saves her from a leopard. They overcome class prejudice and escape to America.

THE SHEPARD OF THE HILLS Harold Bell Wright Story Picture Corp. Dir. Harold Bell Wright. Harry G. Lonsdale, Catherine Curtis, George McDaniel. Rural drama set in the Ozarks, remade several times over the years. See 1928.

TERROR ISLAND (DEEP SEA LOOT) Famous Players-Lasky/Paramount. Dir. James Cruze. Harry Houdini, Jack Brammall, Lila Lee. Mystery adventure. Woman enlists inventor of submarine salvage device to rescue her father from South Sea island natives who want the special pearl she possesses. Underwater fights, magic, lots of diving.

TOM MIX FILM Fox. Title unknown.

WINGS OF MORNING Fox Film Corp. Dir. J. Gordon Edwards. William Farnum, Herschel Mayall, Frank Elliott, Louise Lovely. Drama set in Singapore, British soldier defends a lady's reputation and is kicked out of the service. As a sailor, he is shipwrecked on a desert island, falls in love, fights off pirates, and is restored to the service.

1920

BELOW THE SURFACE Thomas H. Ince Productions. Dir. Irvin V. Willat. Hobart Bosworth, Grace Darmond, Lloyd Hughes. Drama. Maine diver's son is seduced into treasure hunt and suffers delirium. Father chases villains, shipwreck follows. Underwater filming staged by Thomas Ince using special equipment.

THE BEST OF LUCK Screen Classics/Metro. Dir. Ray C. Smallwood. Kathryn Adams, Jack Holt, Lilie Leslie. Drama. Young American woman comes to Scotland, falls in love, and searches with a submarine for lost treasure in the sunken ships of the Spanish Armada. Underwater scenes shot at Catalina.

DEEP WATERS Famous Players-Lasky/Paramount. Dir. Maurice Toureau. Broerken Christians, Barbara Bedford, Jack Gilbert. Drama. Lighthouse builder falls in love with another man's wife; hard-hat diver falls for his boss's wife, is killed in a shipwreck. Underwater scenes.

DRAG HARLAN Fox Film Corp. Dir. J. Gordon Edwards. William Farnum, Jackie Saunders, Arthur Millett. Western filmed at Middle Ranch, Catalina. Cowboy seeks revenge for his partner's death, kills the man and falls for his daughter, who has a map to a lost gold mine. Bandits and gunfights ensue.

GODLESS MEN Reginald Barker Productions/ Goldwyn. Dir. Reginald Barker. Russell Simpson, Helene Chadwick. Drama. A South Seas rover and his estranged son fight over a girl who turns out to be his daughter.

THE HELL SHIP Fox Film Corp. Dir. Scott Dunlap. Madlaine Traverse, Albert Roscoe, Betty Bouton, Dick La Reno. Drama. Daughter takes over her late father's sailing ship, picks up a shipwreck survivor and falls in love with him. In the South Seas, the crew mutinies, burns the ship, lovers escape by raft. Fox chartered an Alaskan Packers sailing ship for scenes shot at sea.

ESCAPE FROM A BLIMP Universal. Scene for an unknown film, possibly *The Lotus Eater*, 1921.

TRUMPET ISLAND Vitagraph. Dir. Tom Terriss. Marguerite De La Motte, Wallace MacDonald, Hallem Cooley. Drama set in California and New York. First time cast and crew were transported to locations by air. Girl falls in love with poor man but marries for money. Poor man becomes rich, drifts off to uninhabited island. On her honeymoon, girl survives plane crash on poor man's island, suffers amnesia, falls in love all over again.

1921

THE DEVIL WITHIN Fox Film Corp. Dir. Bernard J. Durning. Dustin Farnum, Virginia Valli, Nigel De Brulier. South Sea Islands melodrama. Vile sea captain trades in opium, steals an idol from natives who put a curse on him. His wife and child die, his sailor nephew steals his money, then decides to reform.

DANGEROUS HOUR (Released 1923) Johnnie Walker Production. Dir. William Hughes Curran. Eddie Polo, Jack Carlisle Catherine Bennett. Set in Arizona, a movie about making a movie set in Arizona about oppressed miners.

A WISE FOOL Famous Players-Lasky. Dir. George Melford. James Kirkwood, Alice Hollister, Alan Hale. Melodrama. Sailing from France to Quebec, a rich man falls in love and marries. Raising their daughter proves troublesome for the couple.

THE OFF-SHORE PIRATE Metro Pictures. Dir. Dallas M. Fitzgerald. Viola Dana, Jack Mulhall, Edward Jobson. Based on an F. Scott Fitzgerald story, a rich girl falls in love with a pennyless handsome Russian. Trouble ensues involving a yacht and pirates.

THE LOTUS EATER Marshall Neilan Productions. Dir. Marshall Neilan. John Barrymore, Colleen Moore, Anna Q. Nilsson. Novel twist on the shipwreck melodrama; this time a dirigible wrecks on an island. Hero falls in love with one of the islanders, returns to New York, decides life on the island is preferable, and again changes his residence.

MONEY MASTER Newsreel.

ACTION Universal. Dir. Jack Ford. Hoot Gibson, Francis Ford, J. Farrell MacDonald. Western. Cowboy saves girl from clutches of evil saloon keeper who is trying to get the girl's inherited ranch and gold mine. Cowboy is framed and sent to jail but girl perseveres and clears his name.

MY LADY OF THE ISLAND Universal. Dir. Norman Dawn. Edith Roberts, Jack O'Brien

SHALL A MAN MARRY? Fatty Arbuckle comedy.

1922

EBB TIDE Famous Players-Lasky/Paramount. Dir. George Melford. Lita Lee, James Kirkwood, Raymond Hatton, Noah Berry. Adventure by Robert Louis Stevenson. Three losers on derelict ship find a man and his daughter harvesting pearls on an island. Two of them decide to steal the pearls, the third falls in love with the girl. First two meet violent ends, third escapes an octopus and a burning ship and gets the girl.

BEYOND THE ROCKS Famous Players-Lasky. Dir. Sam Wood. Gloria Swanson, Rudolph Valentino. Society girl marries old millionaire then falls in love with younger man, problems ensue. Rich old man finally sacrifices himself to save the young lovers.

DOWN TO THE SEA IN SHIPS Whaling Film Corp. Dir. Elmer Clifton. Marguirite Courtot, Clara bow, William Walcott. Melodrama. Seafaring father insists his daughter marry a Quaker and a whaleman. She falls in love with a man who is neither.

WOMAN, WAKE UP! Florence Vidor Productions. Dir. Marcus Harrison. Florence Vidor, Charles Meredith, Louis Calhern. Comedy drama. Wife tries to keep pace with social wannabe husband, succeeds too well and makes husband jealous.

YELLOW MEN AND GOLD Goldwyn Pictures. Dir. Irvin V. Willat. Richard Dix, Helene Chadwick, Henry Barrows. Young author acts out his adventure tale, pursues lost treasure, fights off villains, gets the girl. Three-masted schooner *Ocean Vance* anchored off Avalon used in film.

1923

THE COVERED WAGON Paramount. Dir. James Cruze. Lois Wilson, J. Warren Kerrigan, Alan Hale. Western. Cast of thousands as wagon trains on the Oregon trail fight off Indians, prairie fires, and scoundrels.

THE TEN COMMANDMENTS Famous Players-Lasky/Paramount. Dir. Cecil B. DeMille. Estelle Taylor, Theodore Roberts, Charles DeRoche. Prologue contains scenes from Old Testament (The story of Jacob's Well was set on Catalina). Main story set in modern San Francisco.

1924

CAPTAIN BLOOD Vitagraph. Dir. David Smith. J. Warren Kerrigan, Jean Paige, Charlotte Merriam. Adventure. Irish physician is exiled into slavery. He and other slaves capture a Spanish Galleon and become privateers. Like many other pirates, he enters politics, ends up as Governor of Jamaica married to his former owner's daughter.

THE FAST WORKER Universal. Dir. William Seiter. Reginald Denny, Laura La Plante, Ethyl Grey Terry. Comedy. Man assumes his buddy's identity and vacations on Catalina with the man's wife and daughter. He falls for the wife's sister and lands in trouble.

FEET OF CLAY Famous Players-Lasky/Paramount. Dir. Cecil B. DeMille. Vera Reynolds, Rod La Rocque, Ricardo Cortez. A man is disabled in shark attack at a yacht party off Catalina. His wife goes to work, jealousy follows leading to death, near death and attempted suicide.

HER HUSBAND'S SECRET Frank Lloyd Productions. Dir. Frank Lloyd. Antonio Moreno, Patsy Ruth Miller, Ruth Clifford. Melodrama in which a scandalous divorce leads years later to a young man's near disaster.

THE NAVIGATOR Metro-Goldwyn Pictures. Dir. Donald Crisp. Buster Keaton, Kathryn McGuire. Comedy involving Buster with a girl he wants to marry. They find themselves adrift on an abandoned steamship that leads them to a cannibal isle. As they are about to become the main course at a barbeque, a submarine rescues them.

THE SEA HAWK Frank Lloyd Productions. Dir. Frank Lloyd. Milton Sills, Enid Bennett, Lloyd Hughes. A wealthy Englishman is shanghaied and sold into slavery. He escapes to become a pirate determined to rescue his beloved from his evil half brother. Filmed at Point Torquemada and Catalina Harbor.

SIXTEENTH CENTURY Harold Lloyd Productions. No record other than it was set in the sixteenth century and filmed at the Isthmus William Wrigley, Jr. had a bit part as a merchant.

THOSE WHO DARE Creative Pictures. Dir. John B. O'Brien. John Bowers, Marguerite De La Motte, Joseph Dowling. Drama. Sea captain relates how he came in possession of a voodoo schooner and fought off a mutinous crew.

WOMEN WHO GIVE Louis B. Mayer Productions. Dir. Jack Holden. Barbara Bedford, Frank Keenan, Renee Adoree. Drama. Bostonian disapproves of his son's marriage plans and has him shanghaied. His daughter, also planning marriage, stows away to escape her father. Storm at sea leads to father's redemption and forgiveness.

1925

HALF A MAN Joe Rock Productions. Dir. Joe Rock. Stan Laurel, Murray Rock. Two-reel comedy made before Laurel teamed with Hardy. Son of a fisherman finds himself at sea with a boatload of Amazons. Fire at sea maroons him and the girls on a deserted island.

(ENGLISH FILM) Maurice Elvey. Footage shot on Catalina for elaborate fantasy.

THE ADVENTURESS Famous Players-Lasky/ Paramount. Dir. Victor Fleming. Tom Moore, Pauline Starke, Wallace Beery. A Jack London melodrama set in the Solomon Islands. Sickly plantation owner is saved by a female soldier of fortune. They fight off fires, cannibals and evil plots and fall in love. Filmed at Catalina Harbor.

AS MAN DESIRES First National Pictures. Dir. Irving Cummings. Milton Sills, Viola Dana. Melodrama. Falsely accused British officer deserts his post and drifts through the South Seas, becomes rich by pearl fishing and falls in love. Villain interferes, trouble ensues, hero is exonerated.

BAD COMPANY St. Regis Pictures. Dir. E. H. Griffith. Madge Kennedy, Bigelow Cooper, Conway Tearle. Melodrama. Heiress and lawyer connive to keep her brother from marrying a gold digger.

BEN-HUR Metro-Goldwyn-Mayer Pictures. Dir. Fred Niblo. Ramon Navarro, Francis X. Bushman, May McAvoy. Silent version of the classic Lew Wallace novel, complete with big chariot race and even bigger sets.

BLUE BLOOD Chadwick Pictures. Dir. Scott Dunlap. George Walsh, Cecillie Evans, Philo McCullough. Melodrama. Butterfly hunter discovers that his beloved's intended groom is a rum-runner. He takes action to save his girl and her father held captive on the smuggler's yacht.

EVE'S SECRET Famous Players-Lasky/Paramount. Dir. Clarence Badger. Betty Compson, Jack Holt, William Collier, Jr. Romantic comedy. French duke plays Pygmalion with peasant girl, she falls in love with another man.

THE KING OF KINGS DeMille Pictures. Dir. Cecil B. DeMille. H. B. Warner, Dorothy Cummings, Joseph Schildkraut. Silent biblical epic released in 1927 and reissued in 1931 with synchronized musical score. Scenes filmed at Cherry Valley and the Isthmus.

THE MAN WITHOUT A COUNTRY Fox Film Corporation. Dir. Rowland V. Lee. Edward Hearn, Pauline Starke. Historical drama. Navy lieutenant renounces the United States in the early 19th century, and is sentenced to life aboard a naval warship. Many years later, Abraham Lincoln pardons him and he dies on hearing the news.

NEVER THE TWAIN SHALL MEET Cosmopolitan Corporation. Dir. Maurice Tourneur. Anita Stewart, Bert Lytell, Huntley Gordon. Melodrama. San Franciscan agrees to care for the beautiful daughter of late sea captain and a South Seas queen. In love, he follows her back to her island where he degenerates. A friend and his former fiancée come and rescue him. The friend stays with the girl.

THE NIGHT CLUB Famous Players-Lasky/Paramount. Dir. Frank Urson. Raymond Griffith, Vera Reynolds, Wallace Beery, Louise Fazenda. Comedy. Confirmed bachelor refuses an inheritance conditioned on him marrying a girl he doesn't know. By chance, he meets her, falls in love, and complicates his life.

OUR GANG COMEDY Hal Roach.

THE VANISHING AMERICAN Famous Players-Lasky/Paramount. Dir. George B. Seitz. Richard Dix, Lois Wilson, Noah Beery. A Zane Grey western set in the southwest. Love triangle between Navajo hero, white lady schoolteacher and Army horse trader, with evil Indian agent thrown in. Buffalo brought to Catalina for the filming were released on the island, their descendants roam today.

1926

THE BLACK PIRATE Elton Corporation/United Artists. Dir. Albert Parker. Douglas Fairbanks, Billie Dove, Anders Randolf, Donald Crisp. Adventure pirate saga. Man and his father are marooned by pirates on a desert island. Father dies, son becomes pirate seeking revenge. He captures a ship, falls love with girl on board who dampens his pirate fun.

A CAPTAIN'S COURAGE Ben Wilson Productions. Dir. Louis Chaudet. Richard Holt, Eddie Earl, Dorothy Dwan. Melodrama on Lake Michigan in 1853. Men on board a becalmed vessel fight over possession of an island.

GOOD AND NAUGHTY Famous Players-Lasky/Paramount. Dir. Malcolm St. Clair. Pola Negri, Tom Moore, Ford Sterling. Comedy aboard a yacht with showgirls, jealous lovers, and trickery.

MONTE CARLO Metro-Goldwyn-Mayer. Dir. Christy Cahanne. Lew Cody, Gertrude Olmsted, ZaSu Pitts, Roy D'Arcy. Comedy. Three American girls win a trip to Monte Carlo and meet men. Royal imposters, mistaken identity, and love add to the mix.

OLD IRONSIDES Famous Players-Lasky. Dir. James Cruze. Ester Ralston, Wallace Beery, Goerge Bancroft, Charles Farrell. Hawaiian surfer Duke Kahanamoku and Boris Karloff play small parts. Historical drama about the frigate *Constitution* in the Barbary Coast wars off Tripoli in early nineteenth century. Elaborate sea battles in period ships off Catalina Island.

THE ROAD TO MANDALAY Metro-Goldwyn-Mayer. Dir. Tod Browning. Lon Chaney, Lois Moran, Owen Moore. A wretched former sea captain runs a Singapore dive and secretly supports a daughter in Mandalay. He visits her and shanghais her lover, saves her from a fate worse than death and dies in the bargain.

RUM RUNNERS DeMille Productions. Dir. Norman Dwan. A prohibition story with rum as the star.

THE SEA BEAST Warner Brothers. Dir. Millard Webb. John Barrymore, Dolores Costello, George O'Hara. Based on Melville's *Moby Dick*. Seagoing brothers fight over girl, one gets his leg bit off by a white whale and vows revenge on the whale and his brother who tossed him overboard.

THE SILVER TREASURE Fox Film Corp. Dir. Rowland V. Lee. George O'Brien, Jack Rollins, Helena D'Algy, Hedda Hopper. Melodrama set on an Italian island. A man hired to guard silver bullion battles with bandits, gets his sailing ship burned, and his love life tangled.

YELLOW FINGERS Fox Film Corporation. Dir. Emmett Flynn. Olive Borden, Ralph Ince, Claire Adams, Edward Piel. Melodrama. Native girl raised as white by a sea captain in Malaysia becomes jealous of an English girl, then learns that she is really in line for a rajah's throne.

1927

THE BLOOD SHIP Columbia Pictures. Dir. George B. Seitz. Hobart Bosworth, Jacqueline Logan, Richard Arlen. Melodrama about a cruel sea captain whose mistreated former seaman seeks revenge. The seaman is clapped in irons but is rescued when the shanghaied crew mutinies. He in turn rescues his daughter, held captive by the captain.

CAPTAIN SALVATION Cosmopolitan Productions/ MGM. Dir. John S. Robertson. Lars Hanson, Marceline Day, Pauline Starks. Melodrama. Young theologian goes to sea aboard a convict ship, tries to save a fallen woman held prisoner. She kills herself, he seizes the ship from the evil captain and converts the convicts.

CATALINA, HERE I COME Pathé. Promotional film shot on Catalina, features the 1927 trans-channel swim.

COME TO MY HOUSE Fox Film Corporation. Dir.Alfred E. Green. Olive Borden, Antonio Moreno, Ben Bard, Cornelius Keefe. Melodrama. Society girl about to be married meets a lawyer, goes to his house, and is seen by a blackmailer. Lawyer kills the blackmailer and refuses to name girl in his own defense. She comes forward, is socially outcast, lives happily ever after with the lawyer.

DEEP CHANNELS Progress Pictures. Hilding C. Anderson.

HOUSE WITHOUT A KEY Pathé. Dir. Spencer Bennett. Aleene Ray, Walter Miller.

THE KID BROTHER Harold Lloyd Corp. Dir. Ted Wilde. Harold Lloyd, Jobyna Ralston, Walter James. Comedy. Small town sheriff's son is told to evict a traveling medicine show, tangles with the performers, catches the crooks, wins the girl.

SEEING CATALINA Fowler. Promotional film shot on Catalina.

SEVENTH HEAVEN (Released in 1928) Fox Film Corporation. Dir. Frank Borzage. Janet Gaynor, Charles Farrell, Ben Bard. Drama romance. Dispirited Paris sewer worker rescues mistreated girl from her sister, falls in love, goes off to war. Returning blinded after the armistice, he finds his true love who believed he was dead. Their faith is restored.

1928

DRIFTWOOD Columbia Pictures. Dir. Christy Cabanne. Don Alvarado, Marceline Day, Alan Roscoe. Melodrama based on Richard Harding Davis story. A prostitute jumps ship as her ship visits an island to escape her pursuing john. Ashore, she falls in with even worse types and is rescued by an alcoholic beachcomber. He sobers up, she reforms, and the two sail off to a new life.

FOX-CASE Movietone. Follies of 1929. Daniel Rollins, Sue Carrol.

FOX FILM Movietone. Sights and sounds of Catalina Island featuring the Hotel St. Catherine.

HER SUMMER HERO FBO Pictures. Dir. James Dugan. Hugh Trevor, Harold Goodwin, Sally Blaine. Comedy. College swimmer and lifeguard saves a girl from drowning, falls in love. She falls for his rival. The two men compete in the big swim meet to see whose frat pin she will wear.

SADIE THOMPSON Gloria Swanson Productions/ United Artists. Dir. Raoul Walsh. Gloria Swanson, Lionel Barrymore, Raoul Walsh. Based on Somerset Maugham's story. Disreputable South Seas drifter Sadie, falls in love with a marine but is hounded by a reformer. She reforms, is seduced by the reformer who then kills himself. She and the marine sail off to a better life.

SHEPARD OF THE HILLS First National Pictures. Dir. Albert Rogell. Alec B. Francis, Molly O'Day, John Boles. Melodrama set in the Ozarks about a gentle drifter called the Shepard who settles in with mountain folk. He saves the hill folk from drought by making the rains come, then confesses that his son, years earlier, had betrayed a mountain man's daughter. One of many film versions.

1929

CONDEMNED Samuel Goldwyn, Inc./United Artists. Dir. Wesley Ruggles. Ronald Coleman, Ann Harding, Dudley Diggs, Louis Wohlheim. Melodrama on Devil's Island. Young man sent to the penal colony falls for the evil commandant's wife when he is made a house servant. Slapped into solitary, he learns the wife is to be sent back to France. But he escapes, rescues her aboard a ship, and returns to the island when the commandant drowns.

DELIGHTFUL ROGUE R.K.O. Productions. Dir.Lynn Shores. Rod La Rocque, Rita La Roy, Charles Byer. Melodrama. A Latin lover turned pirate becomes the scourge of the South Seas. On an island, he falls for an American dancer, kidnaps her lover, and tries to seduce the girl. When her freed lover is indignant, she dumps him for the pirate.

DIVINE LADY First National Pictures. Dir. Frank Lloyd. H.B. Warner, Marie Dressler, Corinne Griffith, Victor Varconi.

FLESH OF EVE Lasky/Paramount. Nancy Carroll, Richard Arlen.

ISLE OF LOST SHIPS First National Pictures. Dir. Irvin Willat. Jason Robards, Virginia Valli, Clarissa Selwynne. Melodrama. Convict aboard a steamer bound for New York falls for a girl passenger. Their ship becomes stranded in the Sargasso Sea, the "Bermuda Triangle," along with many other lost ships, their passengers and crews. New female arrivals to the lost ship colony must be married to prevent trouble, but trouble ensues anyway. Convict and girl escape on a resurrected submarine.

THE MAN AND THE MOMENT First National Pictures. Dir. George Fitzmaurice. Billie Dove, Rod La Rocque, Gwen Lee. Comedy drama. Lady pilot crash lands in a yachting party and is rescued by bachelor tying to avoid marrying a pursuing female. Pilot and bachelor fall in love and marry secretly to foil the plans of pursuing female. After a falling out, lady pilot takes off in a huff with her stowaway husband, crashes again and is rescued by his yacht.

THE RESCUE Samuel Goldwyn, Inc./United Artists. Dir. Herbert Brenon. Ronald Colman, Lily Damita. Adventure. English South Seas trader is saved from angry villagers by native ruler, who is then deposed. Trader sails away with ex-ruler and his sister but encounters a stranded yacht, a jealous wife, and more trouble ensues.

SCARLET SEAS First National Pictures. Dir. John Francis Dillon. Richard Barthelmess, Betty Compson, Loretta Young. Drama. Schooner captain goes ashore in the South Seas to find a little action, falls for a prostitute and the two leave for Shanghai. Their vessel sinks, they are rescued by a passing ship with a mutinous crew. Hero saves the ship and the captain.

SEA FURY Tom White Productions. Dir. George Melford. James Hallet, Mildred Harris, Frank Campeau. Melodrama. Smuggler ship captain rescues sole survivor (female) of shipwreck, his crew mutinies and kills the captain and officers, save one. Survivor agrees to navigate if the girl is spared. They escape and survive big storm.

THE SINGLE STANDARD Metro-Goldwyn-Mayer. Dir. Cedric Gibbons. Greta Garbo, Nils Asher, John Mack Brown. Drama. Feminist believes a single standard of conduct applies to men and women. She rejects marriage with man of her social set in favor of affair with her chauffeur. After his suicide, she yachts off to the South Seas with an ex-prizefighter. Pregnant, she returns home and marries her equal, rejects the lower class prizefighter.

SO LONG LETTY Warner Brothers Pictures. Dir. Lloyd Bacon. Charlotte Greenwood, Claude Gillingwater, Grant Withers, Harry Gribbon. Musical. Eccentric millionaire's two granddaughters in a beach hotel create complications for guests, a singer, and a beauty parlor operator.

WELCOME DANGER Harold Lloyd Corporation. Dir. Clyde Bruckman. Harold Lloyd, Barbara Kent, Charles Middleton. Comedy set in San Francisco. Wimpy botanist gets involved with gangsters, drug pushers, and cops.

1930

ANGLES ON ANGLING Hearst-Fox Metro-tone. Sound newsreel about marlin fishing off Catalina

DANGEROUS PARADISE Paramount Famous Lasky. Dir. William Wellman Nancy Carroll, Richard Arlen, Warner Oland. Melodrama suggested by Joseph Conrad's *Victory*. Female orchestra member flees a man's advances to a South Seas island where she encounters murder and seduction and lust for gold.

DERELICT Paramount-Publix. Dir. Rowland V. Lee. George Bancroft, Jesse Royce Landis, William Boyd. Adventure melodrama. Love, life, and shipwreck on freighters at sea with a woman on board.

HELL'S ISLAND Columbia Pictures. Dir. Edward Sloman. Jack Holt, Ralph Graves, Dorothy Sebastian, Richard Cramer. Adventure melodrama. Two Americans in the French Foreign Legion pursue a cabaret singer across the desert. One ends up on Devils Island.

MEN WITHOUT WOMEN Fox. Dir. John Ford. Kenneth MacKenna, Frank Anderson, Paul Page. Melodrama in the China Sea with a sunken American submarine, rescue by a British ship, and gallant heroics and sacrifice. John Wayne in a bit part.

MOBY DICK Warner Brothers. Dir. Lloyd Bacon. John Barrymore, Joan Bennett, Lloyd Hughes. Seaman has a thing about a white whale after it bites off his leg. Derived from Herman Melville's classic tale, by way of the 1926 silent version, *The Sea Beast*.

THE SEA GOD Paramount-Publix. Dir. George Abbott. Richard Arlen, Fay Wray, Eugene Pallette. Adventure melodrama. Two South Seas traders vie for Daisy, embark on a sea race that leads to pearl diving and cannibals.

DAMES AHOY! Universal Pictures. (Silent, one of the last.) Comedy. Dir. William James Craft. Glenn Tryon, Helen Wright, Otis Harlan, Gertrude Astor. Three sailors chase a dance hall blonde with an unusual birthmark. She ends up catching them.

THE SEA WOLF Fox. Dir. Alfred Santell. Milton Sills, Jane Keith, Raymond Hackett. Romantic melodrama. One of several versions based on Jack London's classic story of "Wolf" Larsen and his hell ship.

SEAS BENEATH (Released in 1931) Fox Film Corporation. Dir. John Ford. George O'Brien, Marion Lessing, Mona Maris. Drama. Schooner "mystery ship" towing an American submarine lures a German U-boat to attack. At a port in the Canary Islands the crew meets and fraternizes with German crew, leading to tragic consequences.

STRANGE BIRDS Mack Sennett Productions

1931

ALOHA Rogell Productions. Dir. Albert Rogell. Ben Lyon, Raquel Torres, Robert Edeson, Alan Hale, Thelma Todd. Melodrama. South Sea island girl prefers an American to a man of her tribe and ends up jumping into a volcano.

CORSAIR United Artists. Dir. Robert Ross. Chester Morris, Alison Lloyd, Fred Kohler. Crime drama. Rejected by tycoon's daughter, a college boy becomes a bootlegger and hijacker on board the yacht *Corsair*.

DANCING DYNAMITE Richard Talmadge Productions. Dir. Noel Mason. Richard Talmadge, Blanche Mehaffey, Robert Ellis, Walter Brennan. Drama. A Catalina fisherman woos a wealthy fish canner's daughter and tries to break into high society. After saving her from kidnappers, he succeeds.

GIRLS ABOUT TOWN Paramount-Publix. Director George Cukor. Kay Francis, Joel McCrea, Lilyan Tashman. Romantic comedy. Two gold diggers meet a rich yachtsman and plan a jewelry swindle that backfires.

MY PAST Warner Brothers. Dir. Roy Del Ruth. Bebe Daniels, Lewis Stone, Ben Lyon, Joan Blondell. Romance

Drama. Rich industrialist invites his girl friend and his business partner to a party on his yacht. They fall in love then break up. John consoles her, takes her to France on his yacht so the lovers can reunite.

GOLD DUST GERTIE Warner Brothers. Dir. Lloyd Bacon. Winnie Lightner, Ole Olsen, Chic Johnson. Comedy. Two clothing mill workers married to twins were married before, each to the same woman. Their ex-wife shows up, complicates things, models risque swimsuits and runs off with the boss.

THE SIN SHIP R.K.O. Radio Pictures. Dir. Louis Wohlheim. Louis Wohlheim, Mary Astor, Ian Keith. Crime drama. Drunken sea captain in San Francisco picks up minister and his wife for trip to Mexico. Minister turns out to be a fugitive and his "wife" a gangster's moll.

BIRD OF PARADISE R.K.O. Radio Pictures. Dir. King vidor. Dolores Del Rio, Joel McCrea, John Halliday. Adventure. Yachtsman in the South Seas falls for a native princess, kidnaps her to prevent her marriage to a chieftain, and incurs the wrath of Pele, the volcano god.

1932

DANGEROUSLY YOURS Fox Film Corporation. Dir. Frank Tuttle. Warner Baxter, Miriam Jordan, Herbert Mundin. Comedy. Rich playboy borrows a friend's yacht to impress his girl, while his buddy uses the situation to steal a diamond necklace and kidnap the girl.

FAST LIFE Metro-Goldwyn-Mayer. Director Harry Pollard. William Haines, Madge Evans, Conrad Nagel. Comedy. Two ex-sailors invent a speedboat engine, get involved with the daughter of a boat builder, and help win a big boat race. Set on Catalina with racing, chases, cops and bootleggers.

THE GOLDEN WEST Fox Film Corporation. Dir. David Howard. George O'Brien, Janet chandler, Marion Burns. Western. Boy and girl escape feuding families and head west, encountering buffalo stampedes, Indian attacks, and badmen. Based on a Zane Grey story.

ISLAND OF LOST SOULS Paramount. Dir. Erle C. Kenton. Charles Laughton, Bela Lugosi, Richard Arlen, cameos by Randolph Scott and Buster Crabbe. Horror story based on H.G. Well's *The Island of Dr. Moreau*. Mad scientist on remote island makes men out of animals. Shipwreck survivor discovers he is to be mated with the "Panther Woman."

THE MATCH KING First National Pictures. Dir. Howard Bretherton & William Keighley. Warren William, Lili Damita, Glenda Farrell. Drama. Chicago scoundrel runs a Ponzi scheme to buy up match factories in Europe. After the stock market crashes, his empire goes up in smoke.

ONE WAY PASSAGE Warner Brothers Pictures. Dir. Tay Garnett. William Powell, Kay Francis, Aline MacMahon. Drama. Convicted murderer being transported from Hong Kong to California falls in love aboard ship and persuades his police escort to remove his handcuffs. In Honolulu he has a fling with his lady unaware that she is dying. Rather than escape, he returns with her to the ship in a futile attempt to save her life.

THE PAINTED WOMAN Fox Film Corporation. Dir. John Blystone. Spencer Tracy, Peggy Shannon, William Boyd. Drama. Singapore saloon singer goes to sea with her brutish lover, gets mixed up with pearl hunters on a South Sea island. After octopus attack, murder, thievery and other mayhem, all works out well.

A PASSPORT TO HELL Fox Film Corporation. Dir. Frank Lloyd. Elissa Landi, Paul Lukas, Warner Oland. Drama. Scandalized English woman in East Africa is interned by Germans after the outbreak of World War I. She marries the commandants son and refuses to be bribed into stealing secret map. Map is stolen by her husband, who confesses, then kills himself to protect his wife.

RAIN Feature Productions/United Artists. Dir. Lewis Milestone. Joan Crawford, Walter Huston, Beulah Bondi, Guy Kibbee. Drama. Cholera quarantines unsavory woman and missionary couple on South Sea island. Woman yields to missionary's conversion efforts and agrees to return to America to face prison for her crimes. Sailor tries to persuade her to escape with him, she refuses, missionary seduces her then kills himself. She returns to her old ways.

TESS OF THE STORM COUNTRY Fox Film Corporation. Dir. Alfred Santell. Janet Gaynor, Charles Farrell, Dudley Diggs. Melodrama. Ship captain wants his maturing daughter to live ashore. He sets up household in a fishing village and finds life on land immensely complicated.

THUNDER BELOW Paramount Publix Corporation. Dir. Richard Wallace. Tallulah Bankhead, Charles Bickford, Paul Lukas. Melodrama. Oil prospector in Central America is betrayed by his wife, who wants to run off with his best friend but changes her mind temporarily when oil man goes blind. After more complications, wife can't make up her mind, so she commits suicide.

TIGER SHARK First National Pictures. Dir. Howard Hawks. Edward G. Robinson, Richard Arlen, Zita Johann. Adventure. Tuna fisherman loses a hand and a crewman to sharks and takes up with the dead crewman's widow. He marries her, becomes jealous of his friend who falls in love with his wife. Angered, he tries to feed his friend to the sharks but becomes shark bait himself.

YOU SAID A MOUTHFUL First National Pictures. Dir. Lloyd Bacon. Joe E. Brown, Ginger Rogers, Preston Foster, Harry Gribbon. Comedy based on the 1927 Catalina Channel swim contest. Man invents unsinkable bathing suit, falls for a girl socialite, gets talked into entering swim competition but is unable to swim. He wins the race by catching a ride on a shark.

1933

THE INTRUDER Director Albert Rey.

THE NARROW CORNER Warner Brothers Pictures. Dir. Alfred E. Green. Douglas Fairbanks, Jr. Patricia Ellis,

Ralph Bellamy, Dudley Diggs. Drama. Man is kept at sea to avoid arrest for murder. He and his companions ride out storm and land on small South Sea island. Man meets girl, jealousy, suicide, false accusations ensue. Another storm leads man and his lover to safety.

THE SON OF KONG RKO Radio Pictures. Dir. Ernest B. Schoedsack. Robert Armstrong, Helen Mack, Frank Reicher. Sequel to *King Kong*. Roaming the seas in disgrace and poverty, captain returns to mysterious island where he captured King Kong and discovers the ape had a son. He finds treasure and feels sorry for the baby gorilla, but his interference costs the son of Kong his life anyway.

THE WORKING MAN George Arliss, Hardie Albright, Bette Davis. A shoe manufacturer shows the children of his late competitor how to run their business.

1934

GRAND CANARY Fox Film Corporation. Dir. Irving Cummings. Warner Baxter, Madge Evans, Marjorie Rambeau. Drama. English doctor who invents an experimental serum fights a yellow-fever epidemic in the Canary Islands. He falls in love with the wife of the island's richest rancher and saves her life.

NO MORE WOMEN Paramount. Dir. Albert Rogell. Edmund Lowe, Victor McLaglen, Sally Bane. Comedy. Two deep-sea salvage divers fight over an insurance saleswoman and another woman, vow "no more women," but to no avail. They get involved in a treasure salvage with an evil captain who plans their deaths. They survive, however, get the gold, swear off women once again.

OCEAN SWELLS R.K.O. Dir. George Stevens.

RED MORNING RKO Radio Pictures. Dir. Wallace Fox. Steffi Duna, Regis Toomey, Raymond Hatton. Adventure. South Seas captain and his daughter are betrayed by swindler first mate who scuttles their freighter to claim insurance on the phony cargo. The captain and his daughter escape to island inhabited by headhunters. They save the chief's snake-bitten son and gain respect of the natives. The captain dies, the daughter falls for the chief's son, they set out to catch the swindler.

SIXTEEN FATHOMS DEEP Monogram. Dir. Arman Schaefer. Lon Chaney, Jr., Sally O'Neil, George Regas. Drama. Girl and her sponge-fisherman lover battle against corrupt competitors to earn a living and pay for a boat. Her drunken father's choice for her future husband proves to be the leader of the corrupt competitors.

TREASURE ISLAND Metro-Goldwyn-Mayer. Dir. Victor Fleming. Wallace Beery, Jackie Cooper, Otto Kruger, Lionel Barrymore. Adventure. Big budget version of classic story of a boy aboard a ship infested with pirates.

WE'RE NOT DRESSING Paramount Pictures. Bing Crosby, Carole Lombard, George Burns and Gracie Allen, Ethyl Merman. A cheery fantasy about passengers and a singing sailor cast ashore from a wrecked yacht on a deserted island. Remake of *Male and Female*.

CALL OF THE WILD Clark Gable, Loretta Young, Jack Oakie, Frank Conroy. Adventure loosely based on Jack London's novel of the same name. Two gold prospectors and their dog in the Yukon find a young woman searching for her husband. With her in tow, they encounter bad men, claim jumpers, and the girl's husband.

1935

CAPTAIN BLOOD First National Productions/Warner Brothers. Dir. Michael Curtiz. Errol Flynn, Olivia de Haviland, Lionel Atwill, Basil Rathbone. Irish physician, exiled into slavery, capture a Spanish Galleon and becomes a privateer, ends up as Governor of Jamaica married to his former owner's daughter. This remake of 1924 silent version includes footage of sea battles from 1924 *The Sea Hawk*.

GENTLEMAN PASSES BY, A Columbia Pictures.

I LIVE MY LIFE (GLITTER) Metro-Goldwyn-Mayer. Dir. Joe Newman. Joan Crawford, Brian Aherne, Frank Morgan. Comic drama. Rich society girl on vacation in Greek islands meets young archaeologist who despises rich people. They fall in love but, back in New York, their relationship gets complicated and contentious. In the end, they return to their island.

MURDER ON A HONEYMOON RKO Radio Pictures. Dir. Lloyd Corrigan. Edna May Oliver, James Gleason, Lola Lane, George Meeker. Detective comedy. Sudden death of a passenger on seaplane to Catalina intrigues amateur female detective. After twists and turns and a second murder she solves the mystery.

MUTINY ON THE BOUNTY Metro-Goldwyn-Mayer. Dir. Frank Lloyd. Charles Laughton, Clark Gable, Franchot Tone, Dudley Diggs. Adventure. Grand scale epic of Fletcher Christian, Captain Bligh, and the famous mutiny. After a miserable voyage to the South Seas with an overbearing captain, followed by a delightful time in Tahiti with the chief's beautiful granddaughter, Fletcher Christian decides he's had enough of the British Navy. Best Picture Academy Award for 1935.

BUDDY ROGER'S PIRATES

PIRATE PARTY AT CATALINA ISLAND

WHEELER AND WOOLSEY

1936

THE BIG BROADCAST OF 1936 Paramount. Dir. Norman Taurog. Jack Oakie, George Burns, Gracie Allen, Bing Crosby, Ethyl Merman, the Nicholas Brothers. Musical comedy. Vying for a prize for the best radio broadcast, an entrepreneur uses a special device that projects on a screen musical acts from all over the world. Plot thickens when love, jealousy and kidnappers intervene. Catalina serves as the mythical island of "Clemente."

CAPTAIN CALAMITY Regal Productions. Dir. John Reinherdt. George Houston, Marian Nixon, Vince Barnett. Drama. South Seas captain, thought to possess Spanish treasure, is pursued by cutthroats. He falls in love, fights off crooks.

COAST GUARD R.K.O. Victor McLaglen.

AVALON, PARADISE OF THE PACIFIC Natural Color Film Studios. Travel film documentary featuring island highlights.

EARTHWORM TRACTORS Warner Brothers. Dir. Raymond Enright. Joe E. Brown, June Travis, Guy Kibbee. Comedy. Hapless tractor salesman wants a big commission so he can marry his girl. He demos the tractor to a hot prospect and causes havoc. He falls in love with the prospect's daughter and pursues her, wrecking her father 's house with the tractor.

HELL-SHIP MORGAN Columbia Pictures. Dir. D. Ross Lederman. Goerge Bancroft, Ann Southern, Victor Jory. Drama. Tuna boat captain in San Pedro picks up drifter and befriends him, then picks up penniless woman, falls in love, and marries her. At sea he discovers his friend is cheating with his wife. Blackmail, storms, and suicide.

ISLE OF FURY Warner Brothers Pictures. Dir. Frank McDonald. Humphrey Bogart, Margaret Lindsay, Donald Woods. Melodrama. A shipwreck lands a stranger on a South Sea island where a newly wed couple dives for pearls. The wife and the stranger fall in love, octopus fights, shootings, and daring dives follow. Stranger turns out to be a detective looking for the husband.

THE SEA SPOILERS

THREE IN EDEN Warner Brothers.

1937

CAPTAINS COURAGEOUS MGM. Director Victor Fleming. Freddie Bartholomew, Spencer Tracy, Lionel Barrymore. Millionaire's spoiled son falls off a boat, gets picked up by fishermen, and befriends one who introduces him to manual labor. For his efforts, the fisherman is killed in an accident, the boy learns a lesson about hard work.

EBB TIDE Paramount Pictures. Dir. James Hogan. Oscar Homolka, Frances Farmer, Ray Milland. Adventure. Based on Robert Louis Stevenson novel *The Ebb Tide*. Renegade and honest man sail a ship loaded with champagne from the South Seas to Australia but renegade hijacks the cargo. Daughter of captain who died from smallpox tries to take back the ship. Storm leaves the crew stranded on small island where an insane man searches for pearls. Schooner *The Golden State* used for the movie.

THE HURRICANE Samuel Goldwyn, Inc./United Artists. Dir. John Ford. Dorothy Lamour, Jon Hall, Mary Astor. Drama. South Sea islander suffers injustice and struggles to free himself from prison. Escaping and returning to his native island, he is restored to his wife and child just as hurricane strikes. He manages to save his family and his pursuers, who then recognize the injustice done to him. Filmed in the South Seas, on Catalina, and an enormous native village constructed on a Hollywood backlot.

SLAVE SHIP Twentieth Century-Fox. Director Tay Garnett. Waner Baxter, Wallace Beery, Mickey Rooney, George Sanders, Elizabeth Allen. Drama. Jinxed ship becomes a slaver before the Civil War, and brings more bad luck to owners and crew. One of the owners falls in love, decides to quit the slave trade and faces an uphill battle.

SOULS AT SEA Paramount Pictures, Director Henry Hathaway. Gary Cooper, George Raft, Frances Dee. Adventure. Abolitionist joins the crew of a slave ship and tries to free the slaves as he had done on other slave ships. Ship catches fire and he tries to save crew in overloaded lifeboat by killing several of them.

SUBMARINE D-1 Warner Brothers Pictures. Dir. Lloyd Bacon. Pat O'Brien, George Brent, Wayne Morris, Veda Ann Borg. Drama. Two Navy officers vie for the same girl and are assigned to a submarine. One of them develops a rescue chamber to save comrades trapped in future submarine accidents. The other one gets the girl.

YOU'RE ONLY YOUNG ONCE Mickey Rooney, Lewis Stone, Ann Rutherford. One of the "Andy Hardy" series. Andy and his family vacation on Catalina where he learns valuable lessons about responsibility and the importance of family values.

THE BUCCANEER (Released in 1938) Paramount Pictures. Dir. Cecil B. DeMille. Frederic March, Franciska Gaal, Walter Brennan, Spring Byington. Drama. Pirate Jean Lafitte sorts out his love life and helps Andy Jackson against the British during the War of 1812.

1938

REBECCA OF SUNNYBROOK FARM Director Allan Dwan. Shirley Temple, Randolph Scott, Phyllis Brooks, Jack Haley, William Demarest. Musical comedy. Over objections of her aunt, little girl becomes a radio star by singing such songs as "The Good Ship Lolipop."

1939

RULERS OF THE SEA Paramount Pictures. Dir. Frank Lloyd. Douglas Fairbanks, Jr., Margaret Lockwood, George Bancroft. Drama. Sailor teams with an engineer and his daughter to build a steamship in the nineteenth century to cross the Atlantic. Sailor falls in love, faces explosions and other difficulties but succeeds.

STUNT PILOT Monogram Pictures Corp. Dir. George Waggner. John Trent, Marjorie Reynolds, Milburn Stone. One of the "Tailspin Tommy" series. Movie stunt pilot Tommy suspects foul play when blanks in his airplane's machine guns are replaced with live ammunition and he accidentally shoots down his buddy.

UNITED STATES COAST GUARD Columbia.

1940

LOVE THY NEIGHBOR Paramount Pictures. Director Mark Sandrich. Jack Benny, Fred Allen, Mary Martin, Eddie Anderson. Comedy. Two feuding radio comedians exchange blows and engage in other shenanigans while chasing a beautiful girl.

ROAD TO SINGAPORE Paramount Pictures. Dir. Victor Schertzinger. Bing Crosby, Dorothy Lamour, Bob Hope, Charles Coburn. One of "Road" comedies with

Crosby and Hope. Two confirmed bachelor playboys head for Singapore, get sidetracked in "Kaigoon," and fall in love with beautiful saloon dancer.

THE SEA HAWK Warner Brothers-First National. Dir. Michael Curtiz. Errol Flynn, Brenda Marshall, Claude Rains. Adventure. Buccaneer insists he is not a pirate because he shares his loot with Queen Elizabeth I.

TYPHOON Paramount. Dir. Louis King. Dorothy Lamour, Robert Preston, Lynne Overman. White girl, marooned on a desert island with a chimp, falls in love with newly arrived beach bum, and triggers bad karma including angry natives, a forest fire, and a typhoon.

1941

FEATHERS

1942

RINGS ON HER FINGERS Twentieth Century-Fox. Dir. Rouben Mamoulian. Henry Fonda, Gene Tierney, Laird Cregar, Spring Byington. Comedy. Bored girl joins two con artists trying to scam a rich man buying a yacht. He turns out not to be rich and loses his life savings to the cons. Girl falls in love with the sucker and helps justice prevail.

1943

GUADALCANAL DIARY Twentieth Century-Fox. Dir. Lewis Seiler. Preston Foster, Lloyd Nolan, William Bendix, Anthony Quinn. War drama based on the best-seller book by Richard Tregaskis. Invasion and capture of Japanese-held island by American marines told through the lives of a few of the participants.

1944

UNCLE SAM, MARINER March of Time newsreel.

1945

ADVENTURE MGM. Dir. Victor Fleming. Clark Gable, Greer Garson, Joan Blondell, Thomas Mitchell. Comedy. Sailor meets a librarian and sets out for adventure.

1947

THE SEA HOUNDS Esskay Productions. Dir. Sam Newfield. Buster Crabbe, Pamela Blake. Serial. Young girl and her father seek hidden gold on an island so they can build a hospital. Bad men try to steal the gold, young man comes to the rescue and the struggle lasts fifteen episodes.

GREEN DOLPHIN STREET MGM. Dir. Victor Saville. Lana Turner, Van Hefflin, Donna Reed, Frank Morgan. Romantic costume drama. Epic romance leads lovers around the world while enduring civil war, earthquake, murder and other discomforts of 19th century life.

1948

CATALINA INTERLUDE Paramount.

MR. PEABODY AND THE MERMAID Inter-John, Inc./ Universal. Dir. Irving Pichel. William Powell, Ann Blyth, Irene Hervey. Comedy. Married man falls in love with a mermaid, hides her in a fishpond and buys a bathing suit top for her. His wife is not amused.

WAKE OF THE RED WITCH Republic Pictures Corp. Dir. Edward Ludwig. John Wayne, Gail Russell, Gig Young. Drama. Sea captain deliberately wrecks his sailing ship carrying millions in gold. Charges against him are dropped and he sets out to recover the gold, encounters bad men, an octopus, a giant clam, pearls and a beautiful girl.

1949

NEPTUNE'S DAUGHTER Metro-Goldwyn-Mayer. Dir. Edward Buzzell. Esther Williams, Red Skelton, Ricardo Montalban, Keenan Wynn. Musical comedy. Swim suit designer and aquatic ballet star encounters a South American water polo team and finds plenty of excuses to frolic in the water.

WHEN WILLIE COMES MARCHING HOME Twentieth Century-Fox. Dir. John Ford. Dan Dailey, Corinne Calvet, Colleen Townsend. Comedy. Eager to fight in World War II, small-town boy enlists only to find himself stuck in small town for years and is ridiculed by townsfolk. Over a frantic four-day period he becomes a war hero in France and returns to disbelief of his family and friends.

1952

CRIMSON PIRATE Warner Brothers. Dir. Robert Siodmak. Burt Lancaster, Eva Bartok, Christopher Lee, Nick Cravate. Lively and humorous swashbuckler about a dashing buccaneer matching wits with a ruthless Spanish nobleman. Lancaster gets to show off his circus background.

ALL ASHORE (SOUND OFF) Columbia Pictures. Dir. Richard Quine. Mickey Rooney, Anne James, John Archer. Comedy. An Army draftee likes to show off for anybody who wants to watch.

1954

MONSTER FROM THE OCEAN FLOOR Dir. Wyatt Ordung. Anne Kinball, Stuart Wade. Roger Corman production of an oceanographer in a diving bell tormented by a big ugly creature with lots of tentacles.

1955

JUPITER'S DARLING MGM. Dir. George Sidney. Esther Williams, Howard Keel, George Sanders. Musical. Temptress tries to prevent attack on Ancient Rome.

THE PHANTOM FROM 10,000 LEAGUES Dir. Dan Milner. Kent Taylor, Cathy Downs, Michael Whalen, Helene Stanton. Oceanographer investigates sightings and attacks by slimy sea monster.

1957

GHOST DIVER

1958

THE DECKS RAN RED MGM. Dir. Andrew Stone.

WANDERER, THE United Artists.

1960

ATLANTIS, THE LOST CONTINENT Galaxy Productions/MGM. Dir. George Pal. Anthony Hall, Joyce Taylor, John Dall. Science fiction. Greek sailor finds princess from Atlantis washed up on shore, follows her to the undersea kingdom and is enslaved. Escaping with his new girl, he brings about a holocaust that destroys Atlantis.

PLATINUM HIGH SCHOOL MGM. Dir. Charles

Haas. Mickey Rooney, Terry Moore, Dan Duryea, Yvette Mimieux. Father investigates son's death at an exclusive military academy.

WAKE ME WHEN IT'S OVER Dir. Mervyn Leroy. Margo Moore, Josh Worden, Ernie Kovaks.

1961

BATTLE AT BLOODY BEACH Associated Productions/ 20th Century-Fox. Dir. Herbert Coleman. Audie Murphy, Gary Crosby, Dolores Michaels. War drama. American civilian in the Phillipines fights off Japanese invaders, his wife, thinking he is dead, becomes guerilla's mistress. American arranges escape from the enemy's clutches, his wife decides to go with him.

WACKIEST SHIP IN THE ARMY Columbia Pictures. Dir. Richard Murphy. Jack Lemmon, Chips Rafferty, Patricia Driscoll, Ricky Nelson. Comedy. Old sailing vessel with rag-tag crew commandeered by the Army in World War II smuggles an Australian spy through enemy waters.

1962

HERO'S ISLAND (THE LAND WE LOVE) Daystar Productions/United Artists. Dir. Leslie Stevens. James Mason, Kate Manx, Neville Brand, Rip Torn. Melodrama set in Colonial America. Settlers find a castaway pirate on the beach who helps them fight off their slave-trader enemies.

THE HOOK Perlberg-Seaton Productions/MGM. Dir. George Seaton. Kirk Douglas, Robert Walker, Nick Adams. War drama. Crew of a gasoline ship during Korean War captures an enemy pilot and is ordered to kill him. Unable to do it, the crew gets to know the man. When armistice is declared, the prisoner panics, tries to escape, and is killed when he is unable to bring himself to blow up the ship.

JACK THE GIANT KILLER (Filmed in 1960) Edward Small Productions/United Artits. Dir. Nathan Juran. Kerwin Mathews, Judi Meredith, Torin Thatcher. Fantasy. Farmer's son in ancient England saves a girl from a giant and tries to escape with her across the sea aided by an imp, a dog and a chimpanzee. They are pursued by a flying dragon, two-headed giant, sea monster and assorted demons.

1963

OPERATION BIKINI Alta Vista Productions/ American international. Dir. Anthony Carras. Tab Hunter, Frankie Avalon, Scott Brady, Jim Backus. Melodrama. During World War II, demolition crew joins submarine crew to locate and destroy sunken American sub to keep its secrets out of enemy hands. On Bikini Island, demolition man falls for female guerrilla.

1964

RAIDERS FROM BENEATH THE SEA Lippert, Inc./20th Century-Fox. Dir. Maury Dexter. Ken Scott, Merry Anders, Russ Bender. Melodrama. Two brothers and two buddies decide to rob a bank. Being divers, they go to Catalina by boat, swim ashore underwater, emerge from the sea and hold up the nearest bank. Returning to the boat, one has a heart attack, the other gets sucked into a steamer's propellor.

1965

CATALINA CAPER (NEVER STEAL ANYTHING WET) Executive Pictures. Dir. Lee Sholem. Tommy Kirk, Del Moore, Peter Duryea. Comedy. Thieves steal a rare Chinese scroll as part of a scam to sell a fake version. The scroll goes overboard off Catalina where two girl-chasing buddies are spending the summer scuba diving. They are enlisted to recover the scroll.

MORITURI Arcola-Colony Productions /20th Century-Fox. Dir. Bernhard Wicki. Marlon Brando, Yul Brynner, Janet Margolin, Trevor Howard. Melodrama. British agent pretending to be Gestapo officer sails aboard German blockade runner in World War II. He tries to deactivate bomb to be detonated in case of capture so the Allies can get the cargo. Survivors taken on board complicate his job.

1966

THE GLASS BOTTOM BOAT Arwin Productions/ MGM. Dir. Frank Tashin. Doris Day, Rod Taylor, Arthur Godfrey, Paul Lynde. Comedy. Young woman whose father runs a glass bottom boat at Catalina falls for a space scientist, her boss. Spies try to steal secret formula, she is suspected by the CIA, confusion reigns.

1967

EASY COME, EASY GO Hal Wallis Productions/ Paramount. Dir. John Rich. Elvis Presley, Dodie Marshall, Pat Priest, Pat Harrington. Comedy. Former Navy frogman dives for sunken treasure and finds underwater competition for the loot. When the treasure turns out to be copper rather than gold, he returns to his former singing career.

THE PERILS OF PAULINE Universal Pictures. Dir. Herbert B. Leonard. Pat Boone, Terry-Thomas, Pamela Austin, Edward Everett Horton. Comedy. An orphan boy falls in love with an orphan girl and vows when they're grown up to return as a millionaire and marry her. When the time comes, he chases her around the world and in outer space from one precarious situation to another.

1968

DAYTON'S DEVILS Madison Productions. Dir. Jack Shea. Rory Calhoun, Leslie Nielson, Lainie Kazan. Melodrama. Group of para-military adventurers plan to steal an Air Force payroll at a base in California. After escaping by truck, they use hidden scuba gear to swim to a boat, where the captain double-crosses them. In the ensuing fight, the scheme comes unraveled.

ICE STATION ZEBRA Filmways, Inc./MGM. Dir. John Sturges. Rock Hudson, Ernest Borgnine, Patrick McGoohan, Jim Brown. Action Drama aboard a U.S. nuclear submarine. Agents rush to the North Pole to recover a downed Soviet space capsule. Others are after the capsule too, including a saboteur aboard the sub.

ROSEMARY'S BABY William Castle Enterprises/ Paramount. Dir. Roman Polanski. Mia Farrow, John Cassavetes, Ruth Gordon, Maurice Evans. Horror. Young wife has a difficult pregnancy and has the devil to thank. Also, her caring neighbors turn out to be witches. Dream sequences shot at Little Harbor and Shark Harbor, on Catalina.

THE LITTLE BUSTARD (U.S.S. BUSTARD) Universal. About a stolen Budda. Filmed partly at Little Harbor.

1969

JOAQUIN MURIETTA 20th Century Fox

PICASSO SUMMER Dir. Serge Bourguignon.

1970

VANISHED Universal.

1971

BLESS THE BEASTS AND CHILDREN Columbia Pictures. Dir. Stanley Kramer. Billy Mumy, Barry Robins, Miles Chapin. Teenagers at a summer camp try to save a buffalo herd (on Catalina) from slaughter.

FIVE DESPERATE WOMEN Robert Conrad, Joan Hackett, Julie Sommars

LITTLE SHEPARD DOG OF CATALINA Arcane Film Inc./Disney. Dir. Hank Schloss. Bill Maxwell, Joe Dawkins, Maynard Quesenberry.

THE MECHANIC MGM/Fox. Dir. Michael Winner. Charles Bronson, Jan-Michael Vincent, Jill Ireland. Drama. Professional killer trains a youth to take over the job.

1972

THE LONGEST NIGHT Universal.

WAR BETWEEN MEN AND WOMEN Columbía Pictures. Dir. Melville Shavelson. Jack Lemmon, Barbara Harris, Jason Robards.

1973

POLICEWOMAN Saber Productions. Dir. Lee Frost. Sondra Currie, Tony Young, Phil Hoover, Jeanne Bell.

SLAUGHTER II American International Pictures. Dir. Jack Starrett. Jim Brown, Stella Stevens, Rip Torn, Cameron Mitchell. Action. Ex-Green Beret seeks revenge for his parent's murder.

1974

CHINATOWN Paramount. Dir. Roman Polanski. Jack Nicholson, Fay Dunaway, John Huston. Dark mystery wherein a detective gradually uncovers unsavory characters, sinister plots, perversions and strange twists. Set in Los Angeles in the 1930s when the city was seeking new sources of water. Catalina's famous Tuna Club appears as the "Albacore Club."

JAWS Universal. Dir. Steven Spielberg. Roy Scheider, Robert Shaw, Richard Dreyfuss. Visiting shark takes a bite-out of a beach resort's summertime profits. Some underwater shots at Catalina.

1977

JAWS II Universal. Dir. Jeannot Szwarc. Roy Scheider, Lorraine Gary, Murray Hamilton. Sequel to *Jaws* in which, four years later, killer shark reappears to ruin beach picnics. Underwater scenes shot at Catalina.

MACARTHUR Universal Pictures. Dir. Joseph Sargent. Gregory Peck, Ed Flanders, Dan O'Herlihy. Portrayal of egocentric general from his retreat from Corregidor in 1942, and his triumphant return, through the Korean War until he crossed President Truman and got fired.

1980

THE MAN WITH BOGART'S FACE Dir. Robert Day. Robert Sacchi, Michelle Phillips, Olivia Hussey, Victor Buono. Detective has his face altered to look like Bogey and gets tangled up in a case worthy of Sam Spade.

1989

THE BLUE MEN Released in 1994. Dir. Denise McKenna. Estelle Parsons. After a family tragedy a young boy is sent to an island to live with his grandmother, where he learns about life, love and understanding.

DICK TRACY Dir. Warren Beatty. Madonna, Warren Beatty, Al Pacino, Charles Durning. Taken from the comic strip complete with good vs. evil, weird characters with funny names. Pick up shots made on Catalina.

1992

BORN YESTERDAY Dir. Luis Mandoki. Melanie Griffith, John Goodman, Don Johnson, Edward Herrmann. Remake of the 1950 classic with Judy Holliday.

1995

MULTIPLICITY Dir. Harold Ramis. Michael Keaton, Andie McDowell, Richard Masur. Comedy. Over committed man has himself cloned into three copies, each with slightly different personality, each adding to his wife's confusion.

SIGHTINGS Paramount.

WATERWORLD Universal Pictures. Dir. Kevin Reynolds. Kevin Kostner, Dennis Hopper, Jeanne Tripplehorn. Sci-fi. World in which humans survive on little floating islands, fighting one another for a place to sit down.

1996

LEADING EDGE

1997

AMISTAD Dreamworks Director Steven Spielberg. Anthony Hopkins, Morgan Freeman. Historical drama about an uprising aboard a 19th century slave ship bound for America. The slaves, once ashore, want their freedom and find a champion for their cause in John Quincy Adams.

BRED AND BORED

MOXIE GIRL

REVOLUTIONARY EYE

1998

THE FINAL DAY

1999

AVALON: BEYOND THE ABYSS Movie made for television, underwater sequences shot at Catalina.

2000

PEARL HARBOR Director Michael Bay. Ben Affleck, Josh Hartnett, Kate Beckinsale. Big budget war romance. Two guys and a girl keep getting tangled up in World War II. Brief fly-over scenes shot on Catalina.

Alphabetical List of Movies

Action, 1921
Adventure, 1945
Adventuress, The, 1925
Adventure of a Madcap, 1915
All Ashore, 1952
Aloha, 1931
Angles on Angling, 1930
Armistad, 1997
As Man Desires, 1925
Atlantis, The Lost Continent, 1960
Avalon, Paradise of the Pacific, 1936

Bad Company, 1925
Battle at Bloody Beach, 1961
Battle of Hearts, The, 1916
Below the Surface, 1920
Ben-Hur, 1925
Best of Luck, The, 1920
Beyond the Poseidon Adventure, 1978
Beyond the Rocks, 1922
Big Broadcast of 1936, The, 1936
Bird of Paradise, 1931
Black Pirate, The, 1926
Bless the Beasts and Children, 1971
Blood Ship, The, 1927
Blue Blood, 1925
Blue Men, The, 1989
Born Yesterday, 1992
Brass Bullet, 1918
Bred and Bored, 1997
Buccaneer, The, 1937
Buddy Roger's Pirates, 1935

Call of the Wild, 1934
Camping Out, 1918
Captain Blood, 1924
Captain Blood, 1935
Captain Alvarez, 1914
Captain Calamity, 1936
Captain's Courage, A, 1926
Captain Salvation, 1927
Captains Courageous, 1937
Catalina, Here I Come, 1927
Catalina Caper, 1965
Catalina Interlude, 1948
Caveman's War, 1913
Chinatown, 1974
Civilization, 1916
Coast Guard, 1936
Come to My House, 1927
Condemned, 1929
Corsair, 1931
Covered Wagon, The, 1923
Crimson Pirate, 1952

Dames Ahoy! 1930
Dancing Dynamite, 1931
Dangerously Yours, 1932
Dangerous Hour, 1921
Dangerous Paradise, 1930
Day at Catalina, A, 1914
Dayton's Devils, 1968
Dead Line, The, 1914
Decks Ran Red, The, 1958
Deep Channels, 1927
Deep Waters, 1920
Delightful Rogue, 1929
Derelict, 1930
Devil Within, The, 1921
Devine Lady, 1929
Dick Tracy, 1989
Down to Earth, 1917
Down to the Sea in Ships, 1922
Drag Harlan, 1920
Driftwood, 1928

Earthworm Tractors, 1936
Easy Come, Easy Go, 1967
Ebb Tide, 1922
Ebb Tide, 1937
Eve's Secret, 1925

Fast Life, 1932
Fast Worker, The, 1924
Feathers, 1941
Feeding Seals at Catalina Isle, 1910
Feet of Clay, 1924
Five Desperate Women, 1971
Flesh of Eve, 1929

Gentleman Passes By, A, 1935
Ghost Diver, 1957
Girls About Town, 1931
Glass Bottom Boat, The, 1966
Godless Men, 1920
Golden West, The, 1932
Gold Dust Gertie, 1931
Good and Naughty, 1926
Grand Canary, 1934
Green Dolphin Street, 1947
Guadalcanal Diary, 1943

Half a Man, 1925
Hell's Island, 1930
Hell-Ship Morgan, 1936
Hell Ship, The, 1920
Hero's Island, 1962
Her Husband's Secret, 1924
Her Summer Hero, 1928
Hook, The, 1962
House Without a Key, 1927
Humdrum Brown, 1918
Hurricane, The, 1937

Ice Station Zebra, 1968
Intruder, The, 1933
Island of Intrigue, The, 1919
Island of Lost Souls, 1932
Isle of Fury, 1936
Isle of Lost Ships, 1929
I Live My Life, 1935

Jack the Giant Killer, 1962
Jaws, 1974
Jaws II, 1977
Joaquin Murietta, 1969
Jupiter's Darling, 1955

Kid Brother, The, 1927
King of Kings, The, 1925

Land We Love, The, 1962
Leading Edge, 1996
Little Bustard, The, 1968
Little Shepard Dog of Catalina, 1971
Longest Night, The, 1972
Lotus Eater, The, 1921
Love Thy Neighbor, 1940

MacArthur, 1977
Male and Female, 1919
Man's Genesis, 1912
Man and the Moment, The, 1929

Man Without a Country, 1925
Man With Bogart's Face, The, 1980
Match King, The, 1932
Mechanic, The, 1971
Men Without Women, 1930
Moby Dick, 1930
Money Master, 1921
Monster From the Ocean Floor, 1954
Monte Carlo, 1926
Morituri, 1965
Moxie Girl, 1997
Mr. Peabody and the Mermaid, 1948
Multiplicity, 1995
Murder on a Honeymoon, 1935
Mutiny on the Bounty, 1935
My Lady of the Island, 1921
My Past, 1931

Narrow Corner, The, 1933
Navigator, The, 1924
Nell of the Notions, 1915
Neptune's Daughter, 1914
Neptune's Daughter, 1949
Never the Twain Shall Meet, 1925
Night Club, The, 1925
No More Women, 1934
Ocean Swells, 1934
Off-Shore Pirate, The, 1921
Old Ironsides, 1926
One Way Passage, 1932
Operation Bikini, 1963
Out of the Darkness, 1915

Painted Woman, The, 1932
Passport to Hell, A, 1932
Pearl of Paradise, The, 1916
Pearl Harbor, 2000
Perils of Pauline, The, 1967
Phantom From 20,000 Leagues, The, 1955
Picasso Summer, 1969
Pirate Party at Catalina Island, 1935
Platinum High School, 1960
Policewoman, 1973
Primitive Man, 1913

Raiders From Beneath the Sea, 1964
Rain, 1932
Rebecca of Sunnybrook Farm, 1938
Red Morning, 1934
Rescue, The, 1929
Revolutionary Eye, 1997
Rings on Her Fingers, 1942
Road to Mandalay, The, 1926
Road to Singapore, 1940
Rosemary's Baby, 1968
Rulers of the Sea, 1939
Rum Runners, 1926

Sadie Thompson, 1928
Scarlet Seas, 1929
Sea Beast, The, 1926
Sea Fury, 1929
Sea God, The, 1930
Sea Hawk, The, 1924
Sea Hawk, The, 1940
Sea Hounds, The, 1947
Sea Nymphs, The, 1914
Sea Spoilers, The, 1936
Sea Wolf, The, 1913
Sea Wolf, The, 1930
Seas Beneath, 1930
Seeing Catalina, 1927
Seventh Heaven, 1927
Shall A Man Marry? 1921
Shepard of the Hills, The, 1919
Shepard of the Hills, 1928
Ship Wreck, A, 1914
Sightings, 1996
Silver Treasure, The, 1926
Single Standard, The, 1929
Sin Ship, The, 1931
Sixteen Fathoms Deep, 1934
Sixteenth Century, 1924
Slaughter II, 1973
Slave Ship, 1937
Smugglers, The, 1914
Son of Kong, The, 1933
Souls at Sea, 1937
Sound Off, 1952
So Long Letty, 1929
Stowaways and Strategy, 1917
Strange Birds, 1930
Stunt Pilot, 1939
Submarine D-1, 1937
Submarine Pirate, A, 1915
Swordfishing With Rod and Reel at Catalina, 1918

Ten Commandments, The, 1923
Terror Island, 1919
Tess of the Storm Country, 1932
Those Who Dare, 1924
Three in Eden, 1936
Thunder Below, 1932
Tiger Shark, 1932
To Have and to Hold, 1916
Treasure Island, 1918
Treasure Island, 1934
Trumpet Island, 1920
Typhoon, 1940

Uncle Sam, Mariner, 1944
Undine, 1916
United States Coast Guard, 1939

Valley of the Moon, 1914
Vanished, 1970
Vanishing American, The, 1972

Wackiest Ship in the Army, 1961
Wake of the Red Witch, 1948
Wake Me When It's Over, 1960
War Between Men and Women, 1925
Waterworld, 1995
We're Not Dressing, 1934
Welcome Danger, 1929
Wheeler and Woolsey, 1935
When a Man Sees Red, 1917
When Willie Comes Marching Home, 1949
Who's Who, 1914
Wings of Morning, 1919
Wise Fool, A, 1921
Woman, The, 1915
Woman, Wake Up!, 1922
Women Who Give, 1924
Working Man, The, 1933

Yellow Fingers, 1926
Yellow Men and Gold, 1922
You Said A Mouthful, 1932
Young Romance, 1915
You're Only Young Once, 1937

Catalina Movie Time Line

(Continued from Page 11)

1910 The Banning brothers, owners of Catalina Island at the time, build a fishermen's bungalow at the Isthmus, later used by movie companies for lodging. The Bannings operate horse-drawn stage coaches to the Isthmus, coaches are later used in movie westerns.

1911 D.W. Griffith discovers Catalina's scenic possibilities, films *Man's Genesis* on the island.

1913 Full-length movies called "Feature films," are developed by Adolph Zukor and others. Studios prosper, making Hollywood the center of movie-making in America.

1914 Mack Sennett's Comedies troupe comes to Catalina to shoot *The Sea Nymphs*, first of several Fatty Arbuckle movies. Catalina's sea lion mascot, Old Ben, appears in the film.

1915 Big fire destroys half of Avalon including Hotel Metropole. Enterprising movie maker Tom Ince films the ruins and incorporates footage in the movie, *Civilization*. First movie filmed at Catalina with extensive underwater photography: *A Submarine Pirate*, starring Sidney Chaplin, brother of Charlie Chaplin.

1918 Fox Film Corporation films the silent version of *Treasure Island*, first "pirate" movie shot on Catalina. Includes scenes shot at the Isthmus. Hotel St. Catherine built at Descanso Canyon, next to Avalon, becomes the favorite of the Hollywood set. Avid fisherman and author fisherman Zane Grey moves to Avalon, becomes acquaintance of western movie star Tom Mix, who also builds a house in Avalon.

1919 William Wrigley, Jr becomes sole owner of Catalina Island, appoints David M. Renton to supervise all construction and concession operations on the island. Director/producer Cecil B. DeMille comes to Catalina to make Gloria Swanson film *Male and Female.* Sid Chaplin opens first air service to Catalina with a three-person seaplane. The service lasts only one year. United Artists Corporation formed in Hollywood by Douglas Fairbanks, Mary Pickford, Charlie Chaplin, and D.W. Griffith.

1920 First "cowboy" western shot on Catalina: *Drag Harlan*, with William Farnum. Tom Mix makes several short westerns on Catalina over the next few years. Hotel Atwater opens in Avalon, becomes popular quarters for movie crews in the 1920s and 1930s.

1921 William Wrigley, Jr. brings his baseball team, the Chicago Cubs, to Catalina for spring training, an annual event until 1951.

1922 Catalina Speed Boat Company starts operation with high-powered "Miss Catalina" boats that, later, were featured in several movies, including *You're Only Young Once*, an "Andy Hardy" movie made in 1937, starring Mickey Rooney.

1923 Director Cecil B. DeMille builds sets at the Isthmus for *The Ten Commandments.*

1924 *Feet of Clay* filmed at Avalon using Hotel St. Catherine as backdrop. Buster Keaton films *The Navigator* off Catalina. Steamship *Catalina* begins daily service to the island, carrying 2,000 passengers at a time.

1925 Stan Laurel (before he teamed with Oliver Hardy) stars in *Half A Man*, filmed at Catalina. Bison shipped to Catalina for the western, *The Vanishing American*, are released on the island, the beginning of a permanent herd. "Our Gang" comedy shot on Catalina by Hal Roach.

1926 *The Black Pirate*, starring Douglas Fairbanks, becomes the first Technicolor movie shot on Catalina. *Old Ironsides*, first big budget movie shot at the Isthmus. Tom White hired by Wrigley to promote movie making on Catalina.

1927 Talking pictures are introduced with synchronized sound. Silent movies fade out. Promotional film, *Catalina, Here I Come*, features the first trans-channel swim from Catalina to the mainland, sponsored by William Wrigley, Jr. Grand opening of the Catalina Island Yacht Club building at Avalon.

1928 Bird Park opened in Avalon Canyon. Exotic birds occasionally loaned to movie companies to add authenticity to "South Seas" pictures. Gloria Swanson stars in *Sadie Thompson*, shot at the Isthmus, based on Somerset Maugham story.

1929 New Casino, combination ballroom and theater, opened in Avalon. Became home to big dance bands of the Swing Era. Hailed as one of the best movie theaters in America, the first built from the ground up to accommodate talking pictures. Stock market collapses, beginning of the great depression.

1930 Musicals, light comedies become popular in the movies.

1931 Seaplane airport opens at Hamilton Cove near Avalon. Quick flights to and from mainland enable Hollywood stars to return home after a day's shooting on Catalina.

1932 William Wrigley, Jr. dies. Philip K. Wrigley, his son, takes over Catalina operations.

1933 Sequel to *King Kong*, called *The Son of Kong*, shot partially at the Isthmus.

1934 *Treasure Island* with Wallace Beery and Jackie Cooper filmed at the Isthmus.

1935 Scenes for *Mutiny on the Bounty* shot at the Isthmus. Bar with sleeping quarters upstairs used by Clark Gable and others becomes "Christian's Hut," popular movie star hideaway in the 1930s. Hotel St. Catherine becomes focus for *Murder on a Honeymoon*, starring Edna May Oliver. Benny Goodman band broadcasts nationwide over radio from the Casino.

1936 David M. Renton retires.

1942 Catalina closed to visitors due to war. Commercial movie making on the island ceases. Big bands and Hollywood stars at the Casino entertain troops stationed on Catalina.

1943 Scenes for war movie *Guadalcanal Diary* shot at Little Harbor, Catalina, under close observation by military. Military training films shot on and around Catalina Island.

1944 Merchant marine James Dougherty brings his young bride Norma Jean to live at Avalon. Later, she becomes actress Marilyn Monroe.

1945 Movie making on Catalina resumes unrestricted. First film is *Adventure*, a comedy starring Clark Gable and Greer Garson.

1946 Catalina's Airport-in-the-Sky opens, first airfield on the island for land planes.

1947 Postwar movies begin using foreign locations, "film noir" becomes popular. Buster Crabbe serial *The Sea Hounds* filmed on Catalina.

1952 Burt Lancaster, starring in *Crimson Pirate*, rejuvenates pirate/adventure movies. Television shows begin to compete with movies as popular entertainment across America.

1953 Seaplane air service reintroduced between Catalina and the mainland.

1954 Science fiction and monster movies become popular. Films with Catalina Island underwater sequences over the next few years include *Monster From The Ocean Floor*, released in 1954, *The Phantom From 20,000 Leagues*, 1955, and *Atlantis, The Lost Continent*, 1960.

1958 Popular television series *Sea Hunt* begins, starring Lloyd Bridges, features underwater scenery of Catalina. Catalina becomes popular location for episodes of television shows such as *Queen For A Day, Truth or Consequences, You Asked For It*, and *The Lawrence Welk Show.*

1965 Hotel St. Catherine razed.

1966 Avalon Harbor featured in MGM movie *The Glass Bottom Boat*, starring Doris Day

1975 The Wrigley family turns over 86 percent of Catalina Island to the Santa Catalina Island Conservancy for permanent preservation.

1977 Isthmus is setting for World War II sequences in *MacArthur*, starring Gregory Peck.

1979 First annual Catalina Island Film Festival held in Avalon at the Casino.

1981 Actress Natalie Wood drowns near her yacht off Catalina Island while on holiday with her husband, actor Robert Wagner and actor Christopher Walken.

1985 Catalina becomes increasingly popular as location for TV commercials and background shots for movies.

ACKNOWLEDGMENTS

Catalina in the Movies is a work in progress to document the relationship between Catalina and Hollywood, and to catalog the many hundreds of movies that have been filmed, at least in part, on Catalina Island. Generous help was given me in accumulating photographs and the list of films. I am deeply indebted to Thelma "Pat" Nolan, a friend now gone, who with Charles Liddell, started the list for Avalon's first film festival in 1979. They searched through old *Catalina Islander* newspapers for all movie related activities on the island. I have received much help from the Catalina Island Museum, Stacey Ott, Director and Jeannie Pederson, Curator of Collections. I wish to thank David Renton, grandson of David M. Renton for graciously sharing correspondence concerning the movies between William Wrigley, Jr. and David M. Renton. Doug and Audrey Bombard and Jay Guion shared their knowledge as did William Delbert, board member of the Catalina Island Resort Services. Harvey Cowell shared his experience of being an extra in the filming of *Mutiny on the Bounty*. Shirley Davy, Avalon City Clerk and Movie Liaison, was helpful with her records. The Santa Catalina Island Company graciously allowed my use of their picture files. Patricia Moore, former Director of the Catalina Island Museum joined me in a week-long search of the Academy of Motion Picture Arts and Science Library, where we were assisted by the special collections research staff. The wonderful people of Avalon have inspired me and kept me going. I thank you all. —*Lee Rosenthal*

Photo credits: (top, center, bottom, left and right are abbreviated as T,C,B,L, and R.) Catalina Island Museum Society: Pages 7T, 7B; 13, 14, 15T, 16C, 18T, 21, 22B, 23T, 23B: 24C, 26, 27TR, 27BL; 28T, 28TR, 28BL; 30CR, 1T, 31CL; 32C, 33T, 37T, 40T, 41B, 43B, 46B, 47T, 48. Chuck Liddell: 2; Lee Rosenthal: 4T, 16C, 20C, 24T, 32B, 36T, 37B, 43B. San Francisco Maritime National Historical Park: 36B, 37B 44, 45. Santa Catalina Island Company: 4B, 17T, 19T, 19B; 20B, 22T, 23T, 23B;24B, 25B, 27TL, 27BR; 28BR, 29, 33B, 38, 39, 40B, 42. Richard Miller, Catalina tiles. Windgate Press: 1, 3, 9, 10, 11, 12, 15B. 16T, 16B; 17, 18B, 19C, 20T, 23, 28TL, 29C, 30T, 30C, 30B; 31B, 31CR; 32T 34, 35, 41T, 46T, 47B.

ISBN: 0-915269-24-4

Windgate Press P.O. Box 1715 Sausalito, California 94966 Telephone (415) 332 0912